T0233919

Computational Modeling of
Human Language Acquisition

Computational Modeling of Human Language Acquisition

Afra Alishahi

ISBN: 978-3-031-01012-5   paperback
ISBN: 978-3-031-02140-4   ebook

DOI 10.1007/978-3-031-02140-4

A Publication in the Springer series
SYNTHESIS LECTURES ON ADVANCES IN AUTOMOTIVE TECHNOLOGY

Lecture #11
Series Editor: Graeme Hirst, *University of Toronto*
Series ISSN
Synthesis Lectures on Human Language Technologies
Print 1947-4040   Electronic 1947-4059

Synthesis Lectures on Human Language Technologies

Editor
Graeme Hirst, *University of Toronto*

Synthesis Lectures on Human Language Technologies is edited by Graeme Hirst of the University of Toronto. The series consists of 50- to 150-page monographs on topics relating to natural language processing, computational linguistics, information retrieval, and spoken language understanding. Emphasis is on important new techniques, on new applications, and on topics that combine two or more HLT subfields.

Introduction to Chinese Natural Language Processing
Kam-Fai Wong, Wenjie Li, Ruifeng Xu, and Zheng-sheng Zhang
2009

Introduction to Linguistic Annotation and Text Analytics
Graham Wilcock
2009

Dependency Parsing
Sandra Kübler, Ryan McDonald, and Joakim Nivre
2009

Statistical Language Models for Information Retrieval
ChengXiang Zhai
2008

Computational Modeling of Human Language Acquisition

Afra Alishahi
University of Saarlandes

SYNTHESIS LECTURES ON HUMAN LANGUAGE TECHNOLOGIES #11

ABSTRACT

Human language acquisition has been studied for centuries, but using computational modeling for such studies is a relatively recent trend. However, computational approaches to language learning have become increasingly popular, mainly due to advances in developing machine learning techniques, and the availability of vast collections of experimental data on child language learning and child-adult interaction. Many of the existing computational models attempt to study the complex task of learning a language under cognitive plausibility criteria (such as memory and processing limitations that humans face), and to explain the developmental stages observed in children. By simulating the process of child language learning, computational models can show us which linguistic representations are learnable from the input that children have access to, and which mechanisms yield the same patterns of behaviour that children exhibit during this process. In doing so, computational modeling provides insight into the plausible mechanisms involved in human language acquisition, and inspires the development of better language models and techniques.

This book provides an overview of the main research questions in the field of human language acquisition. It reviews the most commonly used computational frameworks, methodologies and resources for modeling child language learning, and the evaluation techniques used for assessing these computational models. The book is aimed at cognitive scientists who want to become familiar with the available computational methods for investigating problems related to human language acquisition, as well as computational linguists who are interested in applying their skills to the study of child language acquisition.

Different aspects of language learning are discussed in separate chapters, including the acquisition of the individual words, the general regularities which govern word and sentence form, and the associations between form and meaning. For each of these aspects, the challenges of the task are discussed and the relevant empirical findings on children are summarized. Furthermore, the existing computational models that attempt to simulate the task under study are reviewed, and a number of case studies are presented.

KEYWORDS

computational modeling, first language acquisition, word learning, syntax acquisition, linking syntax to semantics, probabilistic models of language

To Grzegorz

Contents

Preface

The nature and amount of information needed for learning a natural language, and the underlying mechanisms involved in this process, are the subject of much debate: how is the knowledge of language represented in the human brain? Is it possible to learn a language from usage data only, or is some sort of innate knowledge and/or bias needed to boost the process? Are different aspects of language learned in order? These are topics of interest to (psycho)linguists who study human language acquisition, as well as to computational linguists who develop the knowledge sources necessary for large-scale natural language processing systems. Children are the ultimate subjects of any study of language learnability. They learn language with ease, and their acquired knowledge of language is flexible and robust.

Human language acquisition has been studied for centuries, but using computational modeling for such studies is a relatively recent trend. However, computational approaches to language learning have become increasingly popular, mainly due to advances in developing machine learning techniques, and the availability of large collections of experimental data on child language learning and child-adult interaction. Many of the existing computational models attempt to study the complex task of learning a language under cognitive plausibility criteria (such as memory and processing limitations that humans face), and to explain the developmental stages observed in children. By simulating the process of child language learning, computational models can show us which linguistic representations are learnable from the input that children have access to, and which mechanisms yield the same patterns of behaviour that children exhibit during this process. In doing so, computational modeling provides insight into the plausible mechanisms involved in human language acquisition, and inspires the development of better language models and techniques.

This book provides an overview of the main research questions in the field of human language acquisition. It reviews the most commonly used computational frameworks, methodologies and resources for modeling child language learning, and the evaluation techniques used for assessing these computational models. The book is aimed at cognitive scientists who want to become familiar with the available computational methods for investigating problems related to human language acquisition, as well as computational linguists who are interested in applying their skills to the study of child language acquisition.

I would like to thank Diana McCarthy who suggested offering a tutorial on this topic at the 47th Annual Meeting of the Association for Computational Linguistics (ACL 2009), and Graeme Hirst who proposed writing this book based on the tutorial content. I thank Grzegorz Chrupała, Shalom Lappin, Afsaneh Fazly and an anonymous reviewer for their invaluable comments and feedback on this manuscript. I would also like to thank my colleagues at University of Toronto and Saarland University for their scientific input and emotional support. I am especially grateful to

Suzanne Stevenson and Afsaneh Fazly; I have learned about computational modeling of language through years of collaboration with them.

Afra Alishahi
October 2010

CHAPTER 1

Overview

The study of human language acquisition pursues two important goals: first, to identify the processes and mechanisms involved in learning a language; and second, to detect common behavioural patterns in children during the course of language learning.

According to Ethnologue[1] (Lewis, 2009), in the year 2009, there were almost 7000 languages spoken around the world. These languages vary drastically in their sound system, the size of their vocabulary, and the complexity of their structural properties. Natural languages have certain properties in common: they are highly regular in their morphological and syntactic structure, yet many words in each language have idiosyncratic properties which do not conform to the general regularities governing form. Moreover, children who learn different languages go through similar stages (Brown, 1973; Berman, 2004), although languages differ in the way these stages are realized (Slobin, 1973).

Languages are complex systems and learning one consists of many different aspects. Infants learn how to segment the speech signal that they receive as input, and they recognize the boundaries that distinguish each word in a sentence. They learn the phonology of their language, or the auditory building blocks which form an utterance and the allowable combinations which form individual words. They assign a meaning to each word form by detecting the referent object or concept that the word refers to. They learn the regulations that govern form, such as how to change the singular form of a noun into a plural form, or the present tense of a verb into the past tense. They learn how to put words together to construct a well-formed utterance. They learn how to interpret the relational meaning that each sentence represents, or to construct a well-formed sentence for expressing their intention. On top of all these, they learn how to bring their knowledge of concept relations, context, social conventions and visual clues into this interpretation process. There has been heated debate on whether different aspects of language are learned independently, sequentially or simultaneously, and whether specialized formalisms are used for representing each aspect of linguistic knowledge. We will go back to these questions in Section 1.1.

As complicated as it seems to master a language, children all around the world do it seemingly effortlessly. They start uttering their first words around age one. By the time they are three to four-years old, they can use many words in various constructions, and can communicate fluently with other speakers of their native language. The efficiency with which children acquire language has raised speculations about whether they are born with some sort of innate knowledge which assists them in this process, an issue we will discuss in Section 1.2.

---

[1]http://www.ethnologue.com/

Consistent trends have been reported among child learners of different languages and in different societies. One such common pattern is the change in the learning rate of words and constructions: children are slow at the beginning, uttering their first word around their first birthday. Around two years of age, many toddlers learn an average of one word per hour. Other changes in the behaviour of the young language learners have been observed, for example their initial hesitation towards learning synonyms, or second labels for the objects for which they already have learned a word. When learning the structural properties of a language, most children grasp the regularities that govern form and meaning early on, and at some stage generalize them to the new words that they learn, a fact that is demonstrated by the overgeneralization errors that they make (i.e., applying a general pattern to a word or phrase which does not follow that pattern). However, they eventually learn the idiosyncratic properties of words which do not conform to those regularities without necessarily relying on corrective feedback from their parents. These behavioural trends provide cues for identifying the underlying mechanisms involved in child language acquisition.

1.1   LANGUAGE MODULARITY

A central question in the study of language is how different aspects of linguistic knowledge are acquired, organized and processed by the speakers of language. The (somewhat arbitrary) boundaries that break the language faculty into separate "modules" such as word segmentation, phonology, morphology, syntax, semantics and pragmatics, have been historically imposed by linguists who studied each aspect in isolation, and came up with formalisms and processing techniques specific to one aspect and unsuitable for another. However, later psycholinguistic studies on language acquisition and processing suggest that the information relevant to these modules is not acquired in a temporally linear order, and that there is close interaction between these modules during both the acquisition and processing of language.

The language modularity argument is part of a larger debate on the architecture of the brain, or the "modularity of mind." Various theories have been proposed, ranging from a highly modular architecture where each task (including language) is performed by a domain specific, encapsulated and autonomous module and the interaction between modules is minimal (e.g., Fodor, 1983), to a functionalist approach where modules are defined by the specific operations they perform on the information they receive (e.g., Sperber, 1994; Pinker, 1997), with many variations in between (Coltheart, 1999; Barrett and Kurzban, 2006). In this range of views, on the one end language has been proposed to be handled by a highly specific "mental organ", or the "language faculty" (Chomsky, 1965, 1980), and on the other end, language is proposed to be represented and processed using the same general-purpose skills which underlie other cognitive tasks, such as imitation, categorization and generalization (Tomasello, 2000, 2003). Proposals advocating the highly modular view rely extensively on the studies of Specific Language Impairments (SLI) which imply the isolation of language from other cognitive processes (e.g., Leonard, 2000), whereas the highly interactive views refer to more recent studies on the interaction of language and other modalities such as vision or gesture at the process level (see Visual World Paradigm, Tanenhaus et al. (1995)).

Whether discussing the modularity of mind (Big Modularity) or the modularity of language (Internal Modularity), there is little agreement on the definition of a module. One approach is to define modules in terms of their representational autonomy; that is, each module handles a different type of input data, and uses an internally specified representational formalism for storing and processing that input, but the storing, retrieval and processing mechanisms that it uses might be similar to those used by other modules. A different approach defines a module in terms of its procedural autonomy, where the mechanisms employed by that module for performing its assigned task are specific to it, but the representational formalism it uses might be similar to those used by other modules.

The modularity debate has been highly interleaved with the issue of nativism or language innateness. On the topic of language, the main point of interest has been whether humans are equipped with a highly sophisticated module for learning and using natural languages, consisting of task-specific procedures and representations. We will discuss this issue next.

1.2   LANGUAGE LEARNABILITY

Human beings have an unparalleled skill for learning and using structurally complex languages for communication. There has to be a genetic component that accounts for this unique ability of humans, however the extent and exact manifestation of this component is not clear. The difference between humans and other species in this regard might be due to the size and layering of the human brain or to the sophisticated cognitive skills that they use for various problem solving and decision making tasks. However, it has been argued that general learning and problem solving mechanisms are not enough to explain humans' highly complex communication skills, and some innate knowledge is also needed to account for their exceptional linguistic skills (Chomsky, 1986; Pinker, 1994). This hypothesis, known as the Innateness Hypothesis, states that human beings have task or domain specific knowledge that is innately specified by their genetic code, and without having access to such innately specified linguistic knowledge a child cannot learn a language.

In simpler tasks such as learning the meaning of words, the innateness hypothesis has been formalized in the form of a set of task-specific biases and constraints that guide language learners through the task in hand, particularly in the face of ambiguity (e.g., Markman and Wachtel, 1988; Behrend, 1990, see Chapter 3 for more discussion). But it is the acquisition of syntax (or the structural complexities of a language) which has received the most attention from nativist accounts of language learning.

The learnability of natural languages has been one of the most controversial and widely discussed topics in the history of studying language. The nativist view of language learning states that natural languages are not learnable from the linguistic data that is typically available to children (Primary Linguistic Data, or PLD). The main argument in support of this view is the Argument from the Poverty of the Stimulus (APS; Chomsky, 1965), claiming that child-directed data (or PLD) is both quantitatively and qualitatively too impoverished to allow for the acquisition of a natural language in its full structural complexity. This hypothesis was partly motivated by the mathematical work of Gold (1967), which proved that a language learner cannot converge on the correct grammar from an infinitely large corpus without having access to substantial negative evidence. On the other hand, direct negative evidence (or corrective feedback from adult speakers of language) has been shown not to be a reliable source of information in child-directed data (Marcus *et al.*, 1992; Marcus, 1993).[2] These findings prompted nativist theories of language acquisition such as the Universal Grammar (UG) by Chomsky (1981), proposing that each infant is born with a detailed and innately specified representation of a grammar which determines the universal structure of a natural language. This universal grammar would be augmented by a set of parameters, which have to be adjusted over time to the language the child is exposed to.

In response to the nativist view of language learning, alternative representations of linguistic knowledge have been proposed, and various statistical mechanisms have been developed for learning these representations from usage data. Analyses of large collections of data on child-parent interactions have raised questions about the inadequacy of PLD (Pullum and Scholz, 2002; Legate and Yang, 2002). It has been shown that child-directed data provides rich statistical cues about the abstract structures and regularities of language. Moreover, recent psycholinguistic findings which hint at a 'bottom-up' process of child language acquisition have questioned the top-down, parameter-setting approach advocated by the nativists. These findings have resulted in an alternative view of language learning, usually referred to as the *usage-based* or *empirical* view. Advocates of this view claim that children do not possess highly detailed linguistic knowledge at birth; instead they learn a language from the usage data they receive during the course of learning. Usage-based theories of language acquisition are motivated by experimental studies on language comprehension and generation in young children, which suggest that children build their linguistic knowledge around individual items (MacWhinney, 1982, 1987; Bowerman, 1982; Akhtar, 1999; Tomasello, 2000). This view asserts that young children initially learn verbs and their arguments as lexical constructions and on an item-by-item basis, and only later begin to generalize the patterns they have learned from one verb to another. However, the details of the acquisition of these constructions and the constraints that govern their use are not clearly specified. Explicit models must be explored, both of the underlying mechanisms of learning these regularities, and of the use of the acquired knowledge.

1.3   EMPIRICAL AND COMPUTATIONAL INVESTIGATION OF LINGUISTIC HYPOTHESES

Any theory about the exact representation of linguistic knowledge in the human mind and the underlying mechanisms involved in the learning process has to be eventually assessed by neuroscientific studies of the brain. But in spite of recent advances in measuring and examining brain activities, neuroscience is still far from producing any high-level description of how children learn a language. For the time being, researchers have to turn to other strategies to investigate this issue.

---

[2] However, it has been suggested that the language learner can estimate the "typical" rate of generalization for each syntactic form, whose distribution serves as "indirect" negative evidence (MacWhinney, 2004; Clark and Lappin, 2010a).

As an alternative strategy for probing human behaviour when learning and processing language, psycholinguistics provides a variety of experimental methodologies for studying specific behavioural patterns in controlled settings. These methodologies range from eye tracking and preferential looking studies, which are mostly used to examine human subjects' sensitivity to various associations between linguistic knowledge and the visual world, to measuring reading times and task-based performance for estimating language processing difficulties. In the majority of experimental studies of language, one aspect or property of the task or stimuli is manipulated while other factors are held constant, and the effect of the manipulated condition is investigated among a large group of subjects. This approach allows researchers to isolate different language-related factors, and examine the significance of the impact that each factor might have on processing linguistic data. In such set-ups, it is only possible to manipulate the properties of the input data and the task in hand, and the learning or processing mechanisms that the subjects use for performing the task remain out of reach. Moreover, each subject has a history of learning and processing language which cannot be controlled or changed by the experimenter: all there is to control is a time-limited experimental session. Artificial languages are used to overcome any interference that the subjects' previous language-related experience might have on the outcome of the experiment. But the amount of the artificial input data that each subject can receive and process in these settings is very limited. These shortcomings call for an alternative approach for investigating the hypotheses regarding the acquisition and processing of natural languages.

Over the past decades, computational modeling has been used extensively as a powerful tool for in-depth investigation of existing theories of language acquisition and processing, and for proposing plausible learning mechanisms that can explain various observed patterns in child experimental data. Using computational tools for studying language is as old as the onset of Artificial Intelligence (AI). Early models mostly used logic rules for defining natural language grammars, and inference engines for learning those rules from input data. Over the last twenty years a rapid progress in the development of statistical machine learning techniques has resulted in the emergence of a wider range of computational models that are much more powerful and robust than their predecessors. As a result, computational modeling is now one of the main methodologies in the study of human cognitive processes, and in particular language.

Using computational tools for studying language requires a detailed specification of the properties of the input data that the language learner receives, and the mechanisms that are used for processing the data. This transparency offers many methodological advantages, some of which are discussed below.

Explicit assumptions. When implementing a computational model, every assumption, bias or constraint about the characteristics of the input data and the learning mechanism has to be specified. This property distinguishes a computational model from a linguistic theory, which normally deals with higher-level routines and does not delve into details, a fact that makes such theories hard to evaluate.

Controlled input. Unlike an experimental study on a human subject, the researcher has full control over all the input data that the model receives in its life time. This property allows for a precise analysis of the impact of the input on the behaviour of the model.

Observable behaviour. When running simulations of a model, the impact of every factor in the input or the learning process can be directly studied in the output (i.e., the behaviour) of the model. Therefore, various aspects of the learning mechanism can be modified and the behavioural patterns that these changes yield can be studied. Moreover, the performance of two different mechanisms on the same data set can be compared against each other, something that is almost impossible in an experimental study on children.

Testable predictions. Because of the convenience and the flexibility that computational modeling offers, novel situations or combinations of data can be simulated and their effect on the model can be investigated. This approach can lead to novel predictions about learning conditions which have not been previously studied.

One should be cautious when interpreting the outcome of a computational model. If carefully designed and evaluated, computational models can show what type of linguistic knowledge is learnable from what input data. Also, they can demonstrate that certain learning mechanisms result in behavioural patterns that are more in line with those of children. In other words, computational modeling can give us insights about which representations and processes are more plausible in light of the experimental findings on child language acquisition. However, even the most successful computational models can hardly prove that humans exploit a certain strategy or technique when learning a language. We will talk about interpreting and evaluating computational models of language acquisition in more detail in the following chapters.

1.4   THE SCOPE OF THIS BOOK

This book will discuss the main questions that the researchers in the field of computational language acquisition are concerned with, and it will review common approaches and techniques used in developing computational models for addressing these questions. Computational modeling has been applied to different domains of language acquisition, including word segmentation and phonology, morphology, syntax, semantics and discourse. However, the focus of this book will be on the acquisition of word meaning, syntax, and the association between syntax and semantics.

Chapter 2 investigates the role of computational modeling in the study of human language acquisition. It provides a general overview of how computational modeling is used for investigating different views on linguistic representations and procedures, how the theoretical assumptions are integrated into computational models, and what is to be expected from a model. We will briefly introduce the modeling frameworks most commonly used in the domain of language, including symbolic, connectionist and probabilistic modeling. We will also review the available resources and data collections for building and testing computational models of language learning, the empirical techniques of studying language upon which a model must be based, and the evaluation strategies for assessing the success of a computational model in accounting for empirical observations.

Chapters 3 to 5 focus on different aspects of language learning, including the acquisition of individual words, the general regularities which govern word and sentence form, and the associations between form and meaning, respectively. For each of these aspects, we discuss the challenges of the task and summarize the relevant empirical findings on children. Furthermore, we review existing computational models that attempt to simulate the task under study, and take a closer look at a few case studies. A brief summary of the specific learning tasks investigated in Chapters 3 to 5 is given in the following sections.

This book should not be seen as a technical manual: the description of the modeling frameworks, the evaluation techniques and the existing models are deliberately kept at an intuitive level and technical details are avoided. Similarly, it is not meant to provide an exhaustive review of all the relevant computational models that have been proposed in the literature. The main goal of this book is to familiarize the reader with the main research topics that the field of language acquisition is concerned with, and the general trends and approaches in employing computational techniques for addressing these issues.

1.4.1 MAPPING WORDS TO MEANINGS

Learning the meaning of words seems trivial at a first glance: children learn the association between a word form and a concept after hearing repeated instances of the word used to refer to that concept. However, there are many challenges to this seemingly simple task. First, few words are used in isolation, and children usually hear words in a sentential context. Second, a natural language sentence can potentially refer to many different aspects of a scene, and for a language learner who does not know the words yet, it is a challenge to figure out the exact aspect (or relational meaning) that the sentence conveys. Third, child-directed data has been shown to contain a substantial level of noise and ambiguity. Therefore learning the correct mapping between each word and its meaning is a complex process that needs to be accounted for by a detailed model.

In addition to the core problem of learning the word-meaning mappings from ambiguous data, various patterns have been observed in experimental child data which call for explanation. For example, the rate of learning new words by children is not constant: they are slow at the beginning, but towards their second birthday the growth in children's lexicon accelerates considerably (*vocabulary spurt* or *naming explosion*). Another example of a seemingly changing behaviour is the late onset of *fast mapping*, that is, the ability of mapping a novel word to a novel object in a familiar context. These and other patterns have been studied extensively among children of different backgrounds and native languages.

Many task-specific mechanisms have been proposed to account for each aspect of the word learning process. For example, children's fast mapping ability is attributed to an innate bias for naming nameless objects. Others have suggested that the underlying word learning mechanism changes as children grow, and this change affects their behaviour. More recently, a number of computational models have been proposed which demonstrate that many of the observed patterns can possibly be by-products of a single core learning mechanism and the statistical properties of the input data.

In Chapter 3, we will look in more detail at the characteristics of the input children receive for learning words, and their change of behaviour over the course of learning. We will review the proposed constraints and mechanisms for learning words, and the most common computational approaches for investigating these proposals.

1.4.2   LEARNING SYNTAX

Learning the meaning of words is not enough for successful communication: the language learner has to master the regularities that govern word forms, and the acceptable combinations of words into natural language sentences. Natural languages are highly regular in their morphological and syntactic structure. Nevertheless, in each language there are words which do not conform to such general patterns. The challenge of learning morphology and syntax is to grasp the abstract regularities that govern form, as well as the idiosyncratic properties of individual words and constructions.

Chapter 4 reviews different aspects of learning the structural properties of language. The acquisition of inflectional morphology is discussed from the viewpoint of generative linguistics which advocates an underlying rule-based system, as well as alternative views which propose an analogy-based learning mechanism. Further, computational models which simulate each account are reviewed.

Another topic discussed in Chapter 4 is the formation of lexical categories. Categories such as Noun and Verb constitute the building blocks of a grammar, and to a large extent determine the syntactic behaviour of words. A survey of the computational techniques for inducing lexical categories from linguistic data is given, and the evaluation strategies for assessing these categories are discussed.

The rest of Chapter 4 focuses on the acquisition of the syntactic structure of language. This topic has been extensively discussed in cognitive science and computational linguistics. Nativist and usage-based accounts of language are presented, and their computational simulations are discussed, including the nativist parameter-setting models, the connectionist models of syntax, and the statistical techniques for grammar induction from large text corpora.

1.4.3   LINKING SYNTAX TO SEMANTICS

Experimental child studies have shown that children are sensitive to associations between syntactic forms and semantic interpretations from an early age, and use these mappings in producing novel utterances (Bowerman, 1982; Pinker, 1989; MacWhinney, 1995). Children's learning of form-meaning associations is not well understood. Specifically, it is not clear how children learn the item-specific and general associations between meaning and syntactic constructions.

One aspect of language that provides a rich testbed for studying form-meaning associations is the argument structure of verbs. The argument structure of a verb determines the semantic relations of a verb to its arguments and how those arguments are mapped onto valid syntactic expressions.

This complex aspect of language exhibits both general patterns across semantically similar verbs, as well as more idiosyncratic mappings of verbal arguments to syntactic forms.

In addition to argument structure regularities, experiments with children have revealed strong associations between general semantic roles such as Agent and Destination, and syntactic positions such as Subject and Prepositional Object (e.g., Fisher, 1996, and related work). Despite the extensive use of semantic roles in various linguistic theories, there is little consensus on the nature of these roles. Moreover, scholars do not agree on how children learn general roles and their association with grammatical functions.

In Chapter 5, we will discuss the acquisition of verb argument structure, including the theoretical and computational studies of this process in children. Furthermore, we will review the linguistic theories and experimental findings on semantic roles, and the computational models which simulate the process of learning a general conception of roles and their mappings to syntactic constituents in a sentence. Finally, we will look at selectional restrictions or preferences imposed by a verb on its arguments, and the computational models for representing and learning these preferences from corpus data.

CHAPTER 2

Computational Models of Language Learning

In the field of cognitive science, computational modeling refers to using computational tools and techniques in order to simulate a cognitive process, and explain the observed human behaviour during that process. In this book, we focus on developing computational models particularly for the purpose of studying human language acquisition.

In addition to studying a process through simulation, computational models allow us to evaluate existing theories of language learning and understanding, and to make predictions about behavioural patterns that have not been experimentally investigated. However, computational modeling should not be viewed as a substitute for theoretical or empirical studies of language. Section 2.1 focuses on what can be expected from a computational model, and which criteria must be met by a model for it to be considered cognitively plausible.

Section 2.2 reviews the most widely used modeling frameworks for studying language, including symbolic, connectionist and probabilistic. This categorization is more due to historical and conventional rather than theoretical reasons, and it reflects the evolution of the dominant modeling paradigms since the onset of artificial intelligence. A brief overview of each framework is given here (more detailed case studies of models in each group are presented in the following chapters).

Finally, Section 2.3 reviews the available resources and techniques used for evaluating computational models of cognitive processes, in particular of language learning and processing. Unlike more applied systems of Natural Language Processing (NLP) whose performance is measured for a specific task, cognitive models of language cannot be evaluated solely based on a quantified performance metric. A successful cognitive model must not only simulate the efficiency of humans in learning and using language, but also explain the behavioural changes and the errors made by children during that process. Therefore, evaluating cognitive models of language relies heavily on the experimental data collected through the studies of language comprehension and understanding, and on analyzing child-produced data. A brief review of common approaches to analyzing child production data and the experimental methods for studying language comprehension is given in Section 2.3.

2.1 WHAT TO EXPECT FROM A MODEL

Traditionally, linguistic studies of language have been focused on representational frameworks which can precisely and parsimoniously formalize a natural language according to how adult speakers of that language use it. In this approach, the focus is on the end product of the acquisition process, and not on the process itself. On the other hand, psycholinguistic studies mainly emphasize the process of learning and using a language rather than the language itself (Clark, 2009).

This dual approach is also reflected in modeling language acquisition. One modeling strategy is to demonstrate the feasibility of extracting an optimal structure from linguistic input (e.g., a grammar from a text corpus, or a phonetic or lexical segmentation from a large stream of speech signals). An alternative strategy is to replicate the stages that children go through while learning a specific aspect of language, such as vocabulary growth in word learning or the U-shaped generalization curve in the acquisition of verb argument structure. Therefore, it is important to evaluate a model in the context that it is developed in, and with respect to the goals that it is aiming at. We will review the common evaluation techniques applied to computational models of language in Section 2.3.

Another critical point when assessing a model is to identify the fundamental assumptions that the model is based on. When developing a model for computational simulation of a process, all the details of the process must be implemented, and no trivial aspect of the representational framework or the procedure can be left unspecified. However, many of these details are of secondary importance to the process that the model aims to study. It is of utter importance for the developers of a computational model to clearly specify which theoretical assumptions about the implemented model or the characteristics of the input data are fundamental, and which implementation decisions are arbitrary. Moreover, they must show that the overall performance of the model does not crucially depend on these trivial decisions. This point is discussed in the next section, where we overview different levels of cognitive modeling proposed by Marr (1982).

Finally, one has to keep in mind that even the most successful computational models cannot prove that a certain type of knowledge or a procedure is used by children when learning a language. Computational models can only prove that a certain type of knowledge is learnable from a certain type of input data, suggest that some representational assumptions are more plausible than others, or that certain processes or algorithms yield certain behavioural patterns. Cognitive scientists can only use the outcome of computational modeling to gain insight into what is possible and what is plausible, and to verify the suggestions and predictions made by models through further experimental and neurological studies.

2.1.1   MARR'S LEVELS OF COGNITIVE MODELING

Theories of language acquisition and processing can provide a relatively high-level characterization of a process, without dealing with details. When simulating the same process through computational techniques, all the details have to be specified. However, it is crucial for a model to specify where its central claims lie; that is, which level of characterization of the process the model is focusing on.

One of the first (and most influential) categorizations of cognitive models was proposed by Marr (1982), who identifies three levels of describing a cognitive process:

Computational level: identifies what knowledge is computed during the process. This is the highest level a model can aim for: the focus is on what is needed or produced during the cognitive process under study, but any learning or processing algorithm that is used for computing or applying this knowledge remains unspecified.

Algorithmic level: specifies how computation takes place. At this level, the focus is on the mechanisms involved in the computational process.

Implementation level: simulates how the algorithms are actually realized in brain. Therefore, every implementational detail is a vital component of the model.

For example, consider modeling the process of the formation of lexical categories such as noun and verb. A model described at the computational level might focus on the type of information that children are sensitive to, and are likely to draw on for this particular task, such as the distributional properties of the context that a word appears in, or the semantic properties of words. At this level, how this information is compiled and used in forming the categories is out of the scope of the model, and any algorithm that might be used in the computational implementation of the model is of secondary importance and can be replaced by another similar algorithm (as long as the same informational features are used by the algorithm, e.g., the context of the word). At the algorithmic level, a model of learning lexical categories might specify that words are incrementally clustered based on the similarity of their context, and that the clusters are periodically reorganized. However, such a model is not concerned with exactly how the proposed clustering algorithm is realized in the human brain. Such specification is the focus of models at the implementational level.

It is important on the modelers' side to specify, and on the evaluators' side to take into account, the intended level of the model to be assessed. If the simulation of a model aimed at a computational level of describing a process results in a behavioural pattern that is inconsistent with that of children, it might be due to an inappropriate choice of algorithm or other implementational details, and not because the specification of the specified computation itself is flawed.

2.1.2 COGNITIVE PLAUSIBILITY CRITERIA

In the field of natural language processing, many automatic techniques have been developed over the years for extracting various types of linguistic knowledge from large collections of text and speech, and for applying such knowledge to different tasks. In this line of research, the main goal is to perform the task at hand as efficiently and accurately as possible. Therefore, any implementation decision that results in better performance is desired. However, cognitive models of language learning and processing are not motivated by improving performance on a certain task. Instead, they are aiming at simulating and explaining how humans perform that task. Therefore, such models have to conform to the limitations that humans are subject to. In other words, ideally cognitive models of language must be *cognitively plausible*.

Many different sets of cognitive plausibility criteria have been proposed and discussed in the literature. Here we discuss some of the most important plausibility criteria when modeling a cognitive process.

Realistic input data. A model which attempts to simulate a cognitive process has to make realistic assumptions about the properties of the input data that are available to children during that process. For example, a model of syntax acquisition cannot assume that children are being corrected when producing an ungrammatical sentence, since various analyses of child-directed data have shown that such information is not consistently provided to them. Also, when modeling any aspect of child language acquisition, it cannot be assumed that children receive *clean* input data, since the data almost always contain a high level of noise and ambiguity. Sometimes it is inevitable to make simplifying assumptions about the structure of data in order to keep calculations feasible or to focus on one specific aspect of learning. However, if a model makes obviously false assumptions about the input, any finding by such a model might not be generalizable to a realistic situation.

Language-independent strategies. Children around the world learn a variety of languages with drastically different characteristics, such as their sound system or structure. It is highly im- plausible to assume that children use different learning mechanisms for learning different languages. Thus a model of language learning must avoid any language-specific assumptions or learning strategies. For example, a model of learning syntax which assumes a rigid word order cannot be extended to families of languages with a more relaxed word order.

Memory and processing limitations. The architecture of the human brain and its processing ca- pacities and memory resources are very different from those of the existing computational systems. Thus many of the machine learning techniques that are developed for applying on large-scale data sets are not suitable for modeling human language processing. For example, it is very unlikely that children can remember every instance of usage of a particular word or every sentence that they have heard during their lifetime in order to learn something about the properties of language. This limits the scope of the techniques and algorithms that can be used in cognitive modeling.

Incrementality. One of the by-products of human memory and processing limitations is that lan- guage must be learned in an incremental fashion. Every piece of input data is processed when received, and the knowledge of language is built and updated gradually. This is in contrast to many machine learning techniques which process large bodies of input at once (usually through iterative processing of data) and induce an optimum solution (e.g., a grammar) which formalizes the whole data set precisely and parsimoniously.[1]

Although a cognitive model of language is often expected to provide a cognitively plausible explanation for a process, it is the intended description level of the model which determines the importance of various plausibility criteria. For example for a model at the computational level, making realistic assumptions about the characteristics of the input data is crucial. However, conforming to

---

[1]In language processing, there is substantial evidence that even words in a sentence are processed incrementally. That is, instead of listening to the whole sentence and interpreting it at once, human subjects gradually build partial interpretations for a sentence as it unfolds, and even integrate visual cues into the process before they reach the end of the sentence.

processing limitations (such as incrementality) in the implementation of the model is of secondary importance, since the model is not making any claims about the actual algorithm used for the proposed computation.

2.2   MODELING FRAMEWORKS

The first generation of models of language were influenced by early artificial intelligence techniques, including symbolic systems of knowledge representation and reasoning and logic-based inference techniques which were widespread in 1960s. In this approach, the syntactic structure of a language is typically modeled as a rule-based grammar, whereas the knowledge of semantics is modeled through schemas and scripts for representing simple facts and processes. These representations are often augmented by a set of logical rules for combining them and constructing larger units which represent more complex events and scenarios. Early symbolic models of language used sophisticated frameworks for representing linguistic knowledge and inference in a transparent way, but mostly ignored the role of experience; that is, the statistical properties of input and how they affect language learning and processing.

Connectionist models of cognitive processes emerged during 1980s as an alternative to symbolic models. The architectural similarities between the connectionist models and the human brain on a superficial level, and their capacity for distributional representation and parallel processing of knowledge made them an appealing choice for modeling human language acquisition and processing, but the majority of connectionist architectures required heavy training load and demonstrated limited scalability to naturalistic data.

The relatively recent development of machine learning techniques for processing language motivated many researchers to use these methods as an alternative modeling paradigm. Probabilistic modeling allows for combining the descriptive power and transparency of symbolic models with the flexibility and experience-based properties of the connectionist models. We will review each of these modeling frameworks in the following sections.

2.2.1   SYMBOLIC MODELING

Symbolic modeling often refers to an explicit formalization of the representation and processing of language through a symbol processing system. Linguistic knowledge is represented as a set of symbols and their propositional relations. Processing and updating the knowledge takes place through general rules or schemas, restricted by a set of constraints. Each rule might be augmented by a list of exceptions, i.e., tokens or instances for which the rule is not applicable.

As an example, consider the task of learning to form the past tense of English verbs. A symbolic model may represent the linguistic knowledge to be acquired as the following Context Free Grammar rule:

$$V_{\text{past}} \quad \rightarrow \quad V_{\text{root}} + \text{"ed"}$$

where V_{past} and V_{root} represent the past tense and the root form of the same verb. However, this rule does not apply to many English irregular verbs such as *put* and *sing*, therefore these cases have to be learned as alternative and more specified rules, or a list of exceptions, such as:

$$
\begin{aligned}
\textbf{if} \ \ V_{\text{root}} \ &= \ V_{\text{prfx}} + \text{"ing"}: \\
V_{\text{past}} \ &\rightarrow \ V_{\text{prfx}} + \text{"ang"}
\end{aligned}
$$

$$
\begin{aligned}
\textbf{if} \ \ V_{\text{root}} \ &= \ \text{"hit"} \ \textbf{or} \ V_{\text{root}} = \text{"put"}: \\
V_{\text{past}} \ &\rightarrow \ V_{\text{root}}
\end{aligned}
$$

$$
\begin{aligned}
\textbf{if} \ \ V_{\text{root}} \ &= \ \text{"go"} : \\
V_{\text{past}} \ &\rightarrow \ \text{"went"}
\end{aligned}
$$

Following the Chomskian linguistics tradition, symbolic models of language assume that a language is represented as an abstract rule-based grammar which specifies all (and only) valid sentences, based on judgements of linguistic acceptability (Chomsky, 1981). In this view, language processing is governed by internally specified principles and rules, and ambiguities are resolved using structural features of parse trees (e.g., the principle of minimal attachment; Frazier and Fodor, 1978). The influence of lexical information on parsing and disambiguation is often overlooked by these theories. Language acquisition, on the other hand, has been mainly modeled through *trigger-based* models, where the parameters associated with a pre-specified grammar are set to account for the input linguistic data (e.g., Gibson and Wexler, 1994).

Symbolic models of language are often transparent with respect to their linguistic basis, and they are computationally well-understood. However, typical symbolic models do not account for the role of *experience* (or the statistical properties of the input data) on behaviour and are not robust against noise and ambiguity.

2.2.2 CONNECTIONIST MODELING

The idea of connectionist models is based on simple neural processing in brain. Each connectionist model (or *artificial neural network*) consists of many simple processing units (or *neurons*), usually organized in layers, which are heavily interconnected through weighted links. Each neuron can receive many input signals, process them and pass the resulting information to other neurons. Linguistic knowledge is represented as distributed activation patterns over many neurons and the strength of the connections between them. Learning takes place when connection weights between neurons change over time to improve the performance of the model in a certain task, and reduce the overall error rate. A cognitive process is modeled by a large number of neurons performing these basic computations in parallel.

Various versions of artificial neural networks have been proposed which vary in the neuron activation function, the architecture of the network, and the training regime. For modeling language learning, multi-layered, feed-forward networks have been most commonly used (an example is shown in Fig. 2.1). These networks consist of several neurons, arranged in layers. The input and output of the cognitive process under study are represented as numerical vectors, whose dimensions correspond to input units. Such models are normally trained in a supervised fashion: the model produces an output for a given input pattern, and the connection weights are adjusted based on the difference between the produced and the expected output. An introduction to connectionist modelling can be found in McLeod *et al.* (1998), among others.

The training regime in some of the connectionist models has been changed to better match the human behaviour. For example, in the model of Elman (1991) the main task is to predict the next word in a sentence, therefore the expected output from the model is the same as the next received input. Feed-forward models are further specialized for the purpose of modeling language. For example, Simple Recurrent Networks (SRNs, Elman, 1990) employ a context layer, an additional set of nodes which store a copy of the hidden layer from the previous time step. That way, the model has a memory of what happened before and can use this information for processing the next input items in context.

Connectionist models have received enormous attention from the cognitive science community due to the learning flexibility they offer compared to symbolic models, and because they suggest that general knowledge of language can be learned from instances of usage. However, these models are often simplistic and cannot easily scale up to naturalistic data. Moreover, the knowledge acquired by the model is not transparent, and therefore it is hard to interpret and evaluate.

2.2.3   PROBABILISTIC MODELING

Probabilities are an essential tool for reasoning under uncertainty. In the context of studying language acquisition, probabilistic modeling has been widely used as an appropriate framework for developing experience-based models which draw on previous exposure to language, and at the same time provide a transparent and easy to interpret linguistic basis. Probabilistic modeling views human language processing as a rational process, where various pieces of evidence are weighted and combined through a principled algorithm to form hypotheses that explain data in an optimal way. This view assumes that a natural language can be represented as a probabilistic model which underlies sentence production and comprehension. Language acquisition thus involves constructing this probabilistic model from input data.

Many probabilistic models of language are essentially an augmented version of their symbolic counterparts, where each rule or schema is associated with a weight (or probability). For example, Probabilistic Context Free Grammars (PCFG) use a symbolic representation of the syntactic knowl-

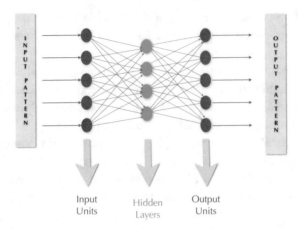

Input Units   Hidden Layers   Output Units

Figure 2.1: An example of a feed-forward neural network.

edge (CFG), but they also calculate a probability for each grammar rule depending on the number of times that rule has appeared in the input (Jurafsky, 1996). However, an alternative (and more radical) probabilistic view proposes language represented as a bottom-up, graded mapping between the surface form and the underlying structure, which is gradually learned from exposure to input data (e.g., Cullicover, 1999; Tomasello, 2003).

In addition to the probabilistic frameworks that are specifically developed for representing and processing linguistic knowledge, many recent computational models heavily rely on general-purpose statistical machine learning tools and techniques. A variety of such methods have been successfully exploited in more practical natural language processing applications. The efficiency of these methods has motivated their use in modeling human language acquisition and processing, in particular for the purpose of extracting abstract and high-level knowledge from large collections of data. For example, one such technique which has been extensively used in computational models of language is Minimum Description Length (MDL), a formalization of Occam's Razor in which the best hypothesis for a given set of data is the one that leads to the best compression of the data (Rissanen, 1978). MDL has proved to be a powerful tool for choosing the best grammar that fits an input corpus. For an overview of the most commonly used statistical techniques for processing language see Manning and Schütze (1999) and Jurafsky and Martin (2003).

The acquisition of linguistic knowledge can be formulated as an induction process, where the most likely underlying structures are selected based on the observed linguistic evidence. The basic idea behind this process is to break down complex probabilities into those that are easier to compute, often using Bayes' rule:

$$P(i|e) = \frac{P(e|i)P(i)}{P(e)}$$

where $P(i|e)$ is the probability of a hypothesis (or interpretation) i given some evidence e, $P(e|i)$ is the probability of e assuming that the hypothesis i is valid (or the likelihood of i with respect to e), and $P(i)$ and $P(e)$ are the prior probabilities of the hypothesis i and evidence e, respectively. The goal of Bayesian inference is to find the hypothesis that maximizes $P(i|e)$.

A family of probabilistic models, generally referred to as Bayesian models, have gained popularity over the past decade (Tenenbaum *et al.*, 2006). In the context of grammar learning, Bayesian methods specify a framework for integrating the prior information about the grammatical structures and the likelihood of the observed word strings associated with each structure, to infer the most probable grammatical structure from a sentence. The prior probabilities are often used for embedding underlying assumptions about the hypothesis space and for seemlessly integrating biases and constraints into the system. It has been argued that prior information (specifically the prior structure over Bayesian networks) is crucial to support learning (Tenenbaum *et al.*, 2006).

Probabilistic models in general are robust against noise, and are a powerful tool for handling ambiguities. A range of statistical and probabilistic techniques have been efficiently employed over the last couple of decades to modeling various aspects of language acquisition and use, some examples of which will be discussed in more detail in the following chapters. However, some suggest that probabilistic methods must be viewed as a framework for building and evaluating theories of language acquisition, rather than as embodying any particular theoretical viewpoint (Chater and Manning, 2006).

2.3   RESEARCH METHODS

As a response to the nativist claims that some aspects of language (mainly syntax) are not learnable solely from input data, a group of computational models have been proposed to challenge this view and show that extracting a grammatical representation of language from a large corpus is in fact possible. These models are not considered as typical cognitive models, since most of them are not concerned with how humans learn language. Instead, their goal is to show that the Primary Linguistic Data (PLD) is rich enough for an (often statistical) machine learning technique to extract a grammar from it with high precision, and without embedding any innate knowledge of grammar into the system. We will look at some of these models in Chapter 4.3. But a typical cognitive model cannot be solely evaluated based on its accuracy in performing a task. The behaviour of the model must be compared against observed human behaviour, and the errors made by humans must be replicated and explained. Therefore, evaluation of cognitive models depends highly on the experimental studies of language.

We need to compare the knowledge of a cognitive model to that of humans in a particular domain. But there is no direct way to figure out what humans *know* about language. Instead, their knowledge of language can only be estimated or evaluated through how they *use* it in language processing and understanding, as well as in language production. Analysis of child production data provides valuable cues about the trajectory of their learning the language. Many developmental patterns are revealed through studying the complexity of the utterances that children produce, the errors that they make and the timeline of their recovery from these errors. On the other hand, comprehension experiments reveal information about knowledge sources that children exploit, their biases towards linguistic and non-linguistic cues, and their awareness of the association between certain utterances and events.

We will look at each of the available resources and common evaluation methodologies in the following sections.

2.3.1   AVAILABLE RESOURCES

Earlier studies of child language acquisition were based on sporadic records of interaction with children, or isolated utterances produced by children which researchers individually recorded. But recent decades have seen a significant growth in the variety and quantity of resources for studying language, and a collective attempt from the computational linguistics and cognitive science communities to use standard format for the expansion of these resources. Some of these resources are listed below:

Transcriptions of dialogues between children and their caregivers. The most well-known and widely used database of this kind is CHILDES (MacWhinney, 1995), a collection of corpora containing recorded interactions of adults with children of different age and language groups and from different social classes. Transcriptions are morphologically annotated and mostly follow a (semi-)standard format, and occasionally, some semantic information about the concurrent events is added to the conversation (e.g., what objects are in the scene or what the mother points to). A snapshot of an interaction session between a child and his mother from the Brown corpus of CHILDES is shown in Fig. 2.2. The English portion of CHILDES has been annotated with dependency-based syntactic relations (Sagae et al., 2010).

Unannotated videos of child-adult interactions. Many of the databases in CHILDES also contain audio or video recordings of the interaction sessions, but these recordings are mostly unannotated. Another massive collection of data has been recently gathered by Roy (2009). Roy has recorded his son's development at home by gathering approximately 10 hours of high fidelity audio and video on a daily basis from birth to age three. However, the resulting corpus is not structured. These collections are hard to use without some sort of preprocessing or manual annotation. Nevertheless, they are complementary to the textual data from the previous group which lack any semantic information.

Annotated videos of child-adult interactions. Some of the audio and video recordings in CHILDES have been annotated by individual research groups for specific purposes. For example, Yu and Ballard (2007) and Frank et al. (2007) use video clips of mother-infant interactions from CHILDES, and manually label the visible objects when each utterance is uttered, as well as the objects of joint attention in each scene. Other social cues such as gaze and gesture are also marked. A more systematic approach is taken by the TalkBank project, which is accumulating the speech corpus of children with multimodal annotation (MacWhinney et al., 2004).

Other researchers have collected smaller collections of annotated videos from children. One such example is the recording of adults reading story books to 18 month old infants, annotated to identify the physical objects and the spoken words in each frame in the video (Yu and Smith, 2006). Another example is a set of videos of a human operator enacting visual scenes with toy blocks, while verbally describing them (Dominey and Boucher, 2005). These resources are sparse, and the annotation scheme or the focus of annotation is rather arbitrarily chosen by the researchers who developed them.

Large corpora of adult-generated text and speech. These corpora, such as the Brown corpus (Francis *et al.*, 1982), the Switchboard corpus (Godfrey *et al.*, 1992), and the British National Corpus (BNC; Leech, 1992; Burnard, 2000) contain large amounts of data, and are representative of language used by a large number of speakers of a language (mostly English) in different domains and genre. Some of these corpora are entirely or partially annotated with part of speech tags or parsed (e.g., Marcus *et al.*, 1994). These corpora are normally used as input data for models of grammar induction.

2.3.2   ANALYSIS OF LANGUAGE PRODUCTION DATA

Ever since the availability of CHILDES (MacWhinney, 1995), child-directed and child-produced data have been extensively examined. Analyses of child-directed data (utterances by parents and other adults aimed at children) have been mainly focused on the grammaticality of the data, its statistical properties, and the availability of various cues and constructions. Such analyses have provided valuable information about what children have access to. For example, an extensive study of child-directed sentences by Marcus *et al.* (1992) demonstrates that children do not have access to reliable corrective feedback (or direct or explicit *negative evidence*) from their parents. Furthermore, child-directed data has been shown to be highly grammatical (e.g., Broen, 1972), and sufficiently rich with statistical information necessary for various tasks (e.g., the induction of lexical categories (Mintz, 2003)).

Utterances produced by children, on the other hand, have been analyzed with a different goal in mind: to identify the developmental stages that children go through in the course of learning a language, and to detect common behavioural patterns among children from different backgrounds. The parameters examined in child-produced data are the size of the vocabulary that they use, the length of the sentences that they produce, the complexity of these sentences (which syntactic constructions they use), the wide-spread errors that they make and the type of these errors, and how each of these factors changes as the child ages. Also, differences between each of these factors have been studied in children of different genders, nationalities and social classes. Such studies have yielded substantial evidence about children's learning curves in different tasks (e.g., word learning or argument structure acquisition).

Properties of adult-child interaction data are directly used in evaluating computational models of language. Statistical properties of child-directed data (average sentence length, distributional

```
2    @Languages:   en
3    @Participants:  CHI Adam Target_Child, URS Ursula_Bellugi Investigator, MOT Mother, ...
4    @ID:     en|brown|CHI|3;1.26|male|normal|middle_class|Target_Child||
5    @ID:     en|brown|PAU|||||Brother||
6    @ID:     en|brown|MOT|||||Mother||
..
9    @Date:    30-AUG-1963
10   @Time Duration:    10:30-11:30
11   *CHI:     one busses .
12   %mor:     det:num|one n|buss-PL .
13   %xgra:    1|2|QUANT 2|0|ROOT 3|2|PUNCT
14   *URS:     one .
15   %mor:     det:num|one .
16   %xgra:    1|0|ROOT 2|1|PUNCT
17   *CHI:     two busses .
18   %mor:     det:num|two n|buss-PL .
19   %xgra:    1|2|QUANT 2|0|ROOT 3|2|PUNCT
20   *CHI:     three busses .
21   %mor:     det:num|three n|buss-PL .
22   %xgra:    1|2|QUANT 2|0|ROOT 3|2|PUNCT
23   *CHI:     no (.) one .
24   %mor:     qn|no pro:indef|one .
25   %xgra:    1|2|QUANT 2|0|ROOT 3|2|PUNCT
```

Figure 2.2: A snapshot of the recorded conversations from Adam database in Brown corpus, CHILDES (MacWhinney, 1995).

properties of words, etc.) are normally used as standard when creating artificial input for many computational models. Additionally, several models have attempted to simulate or explain the patterns observed in child-produced data. We will look at domain-specific examples of such modeling attempts in the following chapters.

2.3.3   EXPERIMENTAL METHODS OF STUDYING LANGUAGE PROCESSING

Evidence concerning what humans (and children in particular) know about language and how they use it can be obtained using a variety of experimental methods. *Behavioural* methods of studying language can be divided into two rough groups: offline techniques, which aim at evaluating subjects' interpretation of a written or uttered sentence *after* the sentence is processed; and online techniques, which monitor the process of analyzing linguistic input *while* receiving the stimuli. More recently, *neuroscientific* methods have also been used for studying the processing of language in the brain. We will briefly review each of these methodologies below.

Offline methodologies. When studying child language processing in an experimental set-up, interactive methods are common in the form of *act-out scenarios* (when the experimenter describes an event and asks the child to act it out using a set of toys and objects), or *elicitation tasks* (when the child is persuaded to describe an event or action in the form of a natural language sentence).

Preferential looking studies are another experimental approach conducted mostly on young children, where their preferences for certain objects or scene depictions is monitored while presenting them with linguistic stimuli. For example, two screens show two concurrent events, a causal and a non-causal action, while a sentence is uttered. The ratio of the subjects looking at one of the events over another can reveal an association between the syntactic structure of the linguistic stimulus and the semantic properties of the action depicted in the "preferred" event.

Online methodologies. A common technique used mostly on adult subjects for identifying processing difficulties is measuring *reading times*. Many factors can affect reading times, therefore psycholinguistic studies use stimuli which are different in one aspect and similar in the others, and measure the reading time of each group of stimuli. This is usually performed through *self-paced reading* (SPR), where a sentence is presented one word at a time, and the subject has to press a button to see the next word.

Another technique that can be used on children as well as adult subjects is *eye-tracking*, where eye movements (or *saccades*) and fixations are spatially and temporally recorded while the subjects read a sentence on the screen. Using this technique, several reading time measures can be computed to evaluate processing difficulties at different points in the sentence. Also, anticipatory eye-movements can be analyzed to infer interpretations.

More recently, eye-tracking techniques have been employed in the *Visual World Paradigm* (Tanenhaus *et al.*, 1995), where subjects' eye movements to visual stimuli are monitored as they listen to an unfolding utterance. Using this paradigm, the construction of online interpretation of a sentence and its mapping to the objects in the visual environment in real time can be studied.

Neuroscientific techniques. Methods for measuring brain activity while processing linguistic stimuli have become increasingly popular. The most common approach is to measure *event-related potentials* (ERP) via electroencephalography (EEG): a stimulus is presented to the subject, while ERPs are measured through electrodes positioned on the scalp. Robust patterns have been observed in the change of ERPs as a response to linguistic stimuli. For example, when presented with a sentence with a semantic anormaly (e.g., *I like my coffee with cream and dog*), a negative deflection is usually observed 400 milliseconds after the presentation of the stimuli (this deflection is called N400). Similarly, a positive deflection is recorded 600ms after presenting a stimuli with a syntactic anormaly (P600). ERP studies have also been used to investigate incrementality in language processing and comprehension (e.g., Kutas and Hillyard, 1983). However, it is difficult to isolate the brain response to a particular stimulus, and it has been a challenge to derive a detailed account of language processing from such data. Functional Magnetic Resonance Imaging (fMRI) is another technique for measuring neural activity in the brain as a response to stimuli. As opposed to EEG, fMRI cannot be used as an online measure, but it has higher spatial resolution and provides more accurate and reliable results.

2.4   SUMMARY

Advances in machine learning and knowledge representation techniques have led to the development of powerful computational systems for the acquisition and processing of language. Concurrently, various experimental methodologies have been used to examine children's knowledge of different aspects of language. Empirical studies of child language have revealed important cues about what children know about language, and how they use this knowledge for understanding and generating natural language sentences. In addition, large collections of child-directed and child-produced data have been gathered by researchers. These findings and resources have facilitated the development of computational models of language. Less frequently, experiments have been designed to assess the predictions of some computational models on a particular learning process.

In this chapter, we reviewed some of the general trends and approaches to modeling language acquisition. We also reviewed the common strategies for assessing a model in the context of the assumptions that it is based on, and with respect to the goals that it aims to achieve. In the next chapters (three, four and five), we will concentrate on more specific examples of language learning problems. We will review in more detail some of the most established experimental findings in each domain, and examine the computational models that have been developed for simulating and explaining these findings.

CHAPTER 3

Learning Words

In the course of learning a language, children need to map words to their correct meanings. This might seem trivial, but the abundance of noise and ambiguity in the input data makes it a difficult task. Child word learning has been extensively studied, and many common behavioural patterns have been observed among children of different backgrounds. Many studies of child word learning show a behavioural shift during the course of learning, or a change in the rate of learning new words.

Various word learning mechanisms have been proposed, ranging from simple associative methods to detailed, task-specific constraints and principles for guiding the child during this process. However, it has proved to be a challenge to develop a single theoretical model of the learning process that explains the impressive efficiency with which children learn word meanings from ambiguous contexts, and accounts for their changing behaviour. However, computational models have been extensively used in order to evaluate the proposed word learning mechanisms, and to investigate whether applying these mechanisms on naturalistic data yields the same behavioural patterns observed in children.

In this chapter, we will look more closely at the challenges of word learning, the empirical findings on children learning words, and some of the suggested learning mechanisms. We review existing computational models of word learning, and examine more carefully a few case studies which are representative of different modeling approaches to word learning. Finally, we look at some recent attempts at incorporating additional information sources into word learning.

3.1 MAPPING WORDS TO MEANINGS

It might seem at first glance that for a child to learn the meaning of a word, it suffices for the parent to point at the referent for that word while uttering it. However, few words are learned in isolation: in a typical scenario, a child hears words in an (often noisy) sentential context (Carey, 1978). The word learner then has to figure out which part of the sentence refers to which part of the event that the sentence is describing.

Sentential context is not the only source of ambiguity when learning the meaning of words. Another well-known problem in word learning is that of *referential uncertainty* (or *referential indeterminacy*), in which the child may perceive many aspects of the scene that are unrelated to the perceived utterance (e.g., Quine, 1960; Gleitman, 1990). For example, when the speaker utters *Mom put toys in boxes*, the child may also form a mental representation of the description of various toys in the scene, of the events of Mom picking up and moving toys, and even of unrelated entities and events such as a kitten playing with a string. In contrast, many utterances that a child hears refer to events which are not immediately perceivable. For example, the child cannot directly map the utterance *Daddy has gone to work* to an observable event or scene.

On top of the complications that arise from noise and ambiguity in the input data, it has been argued that the meaning of certain verbs or situations cannot be disambiguated even through repeated observation of the corresponding event. For example, Gleitman (1990) argues that paired verbs such as *buy* and *sell*, or *chase* and *flee*, can always be used to describe two sides of the same event. Therefore, just by watching a chasing scene, it is impossible for the child to decide whether the verb describing the scene means "chase" or "flee".

3.1.1   CHILD DEVELOPMENTAL PATTERNS

Psycholinguistic studies have attempted to explain children's impressive efficiency in acquiring a lexicon through examining specific patterns that are observed in the course of word learning. We will examine some of these patterns here.

Frequency effects: Experimental studies of word learning show a high correlation between the frequency of usage of a word in mothers' speech and the age of acquisition of the word (e.g., Huttenlocher *et al.*, 1991; Schachter, 1979).

Honing of linguistic form. Young children show difficulty in learning distinct meanings for words which sound similar. However, they gradually learn to discriminate such similar-sounding word forms and to map them to different meanings (Stager and Werker, 1997; Werker *et al.*, 2002; Regier, 2005).

Honing of meaning. Young children are reluctant to generalize a label that they have learned for an object to other objects of the same category (e.g., with the same shape but different colour or size), but older children readily generalize novel names to similar referents (Woodward *et al.*, 1994; Landau *et al.*, 1998; Smith *et al.*, 2002).

Vocabulary spurt: Longitudinal studies of early vocabulary growth in children have shown that vocabulary learning is slow at the very early stages of learning (e.g., 2-3 words per week among 12 to 16-month-olds), then proceeds to a rapid pace (around 10-40 words per week among 18 to 22-month-olds). The learning rate often accelerates when the child has learned to produce about 50 words (e.g., Kamhi, 1986; Reznick and Goldfield, 1992).

Fast mapping: It has been shown that children as young as two years of age can correctly and consistently map a novel word to a novel object in the presence of other familiar objects (Carey and Bartlett, 1978). This behaviour is in line with the observation that children become more efficient word learners later in time (e.g., Woodward *et al.*, 1994).

Acquisition of second labels: Empirical findings show that even though children are generally good at mapping novel words to novel meanings, they exhibit difficulty in learning homonymous and synonymous words which require the acquisition of one-to-many and many-to-one mappings, respectively (e.g., Littschwager and Markman, 1994; Mazzocco, 1997).

Learning stability: Children in normal conditions who are exposed to the same language consistently converge to the same lexicon (i.e., learning the same meanings for the same words). Psycholinguistic studies have shown that the socioeconomic and literacy status of mothers affect the quantity and the properties of the mothers' speech directed to their children (Schachter, 1979; Ninio, 1980; Pan *et al.*, 2005), and this in turn affects the pattern of vocabulary production in the children. However, despite receiving different input data from their environment, an average six-year-old child knows over 14,000 words (Carey, 1978; Clark, 2009).

3.1.2 SUGGESTED LEARNING MECHANISMS

Some consider early stages of word learning to be based on simple *associative learning*, where a child associates a word with a concept upon repeatedly hearing the word used in the presence of that concept (e.g., Smith, 2000). Others suggest *referential learning* to be the underlying mechanism for mapping words to meanings, i.e., children use a variety of attention mechanisms to narrow down the interpretation of an utterance and focus on the referents of the words (e.g., Carpenter *et al.*, 1998; Bloom, 2000). However, both of these mechanisms only apply to cases where a deliberate dialogue is taking place between a child and her caretaker, and do not explain learning from the vast amount of noisy and ambiguous input that children receive from their environment (see Hoff and Naigles, 2002).

An alternative mechanism for learning word meanings from large collections of ambiguous data is *cross-situational learning* (Quine, 1960; Pinker, 1989). It has been suggested that children learn the meanings of words by observing the regularities across different situations in which a word is used. Experimental studies on children and adult learners have shown that both groups are sensitive to co-occurrence statistics, and can efficiently use it to deduce the correct meanings of novel words in ambiguous situations (Smith and Yu, 2007; Monaghan and Mattock, 2009). However, this hypothesis does not explain some of the developmental patterns (e.g., fast mapping) observed in children.

To account for these patterns, many researchers have suggested that in addition to cross-situational evidence, children rely on specialized word learning mechanisms in the form of a set of mental biases and constraints (e.g., Behrend, 1990). A variety of such biases have been proposed, each accounting for one specific observed pattern. For example, fast mapping has been attributed to a principle of the mutual exclusivity of word meanings (Markman and Wachtel, 1988) or to a bias towards finding names for nameless objects (Golinkoff *et al.*, 1992). The delayed onset of vocabulary spurt and the initial reluctance towards learning second labels for objects, on the other hand, have been attributed to a change in the underlying learning mechanism (from associative to referential, for example) (e.g., Kamhi, 1986; Behrend, 1990).

3.2   EXISTING COMPUTATIONAL MODELS OF WORD LEARNING

Computational modeling has been used as a powerful tool for the investigation of the hypothesized mechanisms of word learning. By simulating a suggested theory or learning mechanism through computational implementation, it can be examined whether it can account for learning the meanings of words from realistic data, and for displaying a pattern of behaviour similar to those observed in children.

Several computational models of word learning have been proposed in the literature, with the common goal of simulating the process of acquiring a lexicon by children. However, these models differ widely in their assumptions about the input data, the underlying learning mechanisms that they employ, and the behavioural patterns that they simulate. On a high level, we can distinguish two main groups of models: those which study the association of words and meanings in isolation, and those which study word learning in a sentential context. We will briefly review each group here.

Learning word-meaning mappings in isolation. The associative (connectionist) models of Plunkett et al. (1992), Schafer and Mareschal (2001) and Regier (2005) among others, learn to associate labels (or word forms) to referents (or meanings). In all these models, the input data consists of pairings of a distributional representation of the word form (usually including phonetic features) with a distributed representation of the referent of the word. The referent might be an image (e.g., Plunkett et al., 1992), or a feature representation of the meaning (e.g., Regier, 2005). These models show a pattern similar to the vocabulary spurt observed in children, and gradual sensitivity to the phonological properties of the word form. The model of Regier (2005) also simulates the increased sensitivity to meaning distinctions (e.g., shape bias), and the facilitation of learning second labels for familiar objects. We will look at this model in more detail in Section 3.2.1.

Li et al. (2004, 2007) simulate vocabulary spurt and age of acquisition effects in an incremental associative model. To reduce the interference effect often observed in connectionist models, they specifically incorporate two modes of learning: an initial map organization mode and a second incremental clustering mode to account for vocabulary growth. Horst et al. (2006) focus on fast mapping within a connectionist model of word learning, and show that the behaviour of their computational model matches child experimental data (as reported in a study by the same authors, Horst and Samuelson (2008)). However, the learning capacity of their model is limited, and the fast mapping experiments are performed on a very small vocabulary.

Other models which study word learning in isolation include the competition-based models of MacWhinney (1989) and Merriman (1999). The competition model uses a feature representation of the referent, and determines the activation of a feature set (i.e., a referent) for each of the lexical choices based on the sum of the association of the individual features previously seen with each word. This strategy yields a mutual exclusivity effect, and accounts for the reluctance to learn second labels.

Learning words from sentential context. The symbolic, rule-based model of Siskind (1996) is the first to simulate the process of learning word meanings from ambiguous contexts and in the presence of noise and referential uncertainty. The model uses cross-situational evidence in conjunction with a set of specific word-learning principles to constrain hypotheses about the meaning of each word. In simulations of word learning on artificially-generated input, the model exhibits various behavioural patterns observed in children, such as a sudden increase in the rate of vocabulary growth and the acceleration of word learning with exposure to more input. However, the rule-based nature of the model makes it less robust against noise. (We will review this model in more detail in Section 3.2.2.) Fleischman and Roy (2005) focus on determining which aspect of an event is being described by an utterance, in forming the word-to-meaning mappings in an expectation-maximization framework. For example, their system determines whether an utterance is describing an action such as "get axe", or a subcomponent of that action such as "find axe."

Other computational models incorporate probabilistic interpretations of the cross-situational inference mechanism (Yu, 2005; Frank *et al.*, 2007; Fazly *et al.*, 2010). For example, the word learning model of Yu (2005) uses an existing algorithm (Brown *et al.*, 1993) to model word-meaning mapping as a probabilistic language translation problem. This model is tested on transcripts of the recorded interactions between adults and children, consisting of a limited vocabulary and with no noise or referential uncertainty. Frank *et al.* (2007) propose a Bayesian model of cross-situational word learning that can also learn which social cues are relevant to determining references of words. Using only domain-general probabilistic learning mechanisms, their model can explain various phenomena such as fast mapping and social generalization. However, their experiments are also performed on a small corpus containing a very limited vocabulary. The model of Fazly *et al.* (2010) uses an incremental probabilistic algorithm which learns from pairings of utterances and scene representations, where the input utterances are taken from child-directed speech in CHILDES, and the scene representation is artificially constructed (with a substantial level of added noise and referential uncertainty). Their experimental results show that the model can reliably learn a large vocabulary even in the presence of noise, and can explain various behavioural patterns such as vocabulary spurt, fast mapping, and learning synonymy and homonymy.

While each of the existing models of word learning investigates an interesting aspect of word learning, none of them uses a fully naturalistic representation of the input data that children receive for this task. The first group of models drastically simplify the problem by assuming access to pairs of isolated word-referent mappings, and ignoring the sentential context. The second group, on the other hand, mostly ignore the phonological properties of words and the semantic properties of the referents, and use sets of symbols for representing utterances and events. Moreover, many of these word learning models do not conform to the cognitive plausibility criteria, in particular incrementality. The models of Regier (2005), Yu (2005) and Li *et al.* (2007) among others use batch algorithms which require iterative processing of the whole data set.

3.2.1   CASE STUDY: ASSOCIATING PHONOLOGICAL FORMS WITH CONCEPTS

LEX (Lexicon as EXamplars), proposed by Regier (2005), is an associative exemplar-based model that accounts for a number of phenomena in children's word learning. The main motivation behind this model is to account for children's simultaneous improvement in several aspects of word learning, including the ease of learning, the honing of linguistic form and meaning, and the acquisition of second labels, as described in Section 3.1.1.

The input to the model is a collection of word forms paired with their referents, both represented as feature vectors. The dimensions of the form and meaning spaces represent phonological or semantic features, where some of these features are communicatively significant and some of them are not. For example, the voicing features are significant in English but the pitch is not. Similarly, the shape features are usually significant in identifying labels for objects, but the size or colour are usually not. The goal of the model is to learn the correct associations between form and meaning exemplars, but also to identify which dimensions of form and of meaning are communicatively significant.

Fig. 3.1 shows the architecture of the model. The Form and Meaning layers can act as input or output layers each: given a word form, the model produces a probability distribution over associated meaning exemplars, and vice versa. Each hidden layer stores the already encountered exemplars of form or meaning, and the form and meaning exemplar nodes are directly associated with each other. Learning takes place through adjusting two sets of weights. The associative weights determine the degree of association between any pairs of form-meaning exemplars. The attention weights, on the other hand, encode the selective attention to each dimension of form and each dimension of meaning. The model is trained under gradient descent in error on a training set of words forms paired with their referents, where a pattern over communicatively significant dimensions of form is predictive of patterns over significant dimensions of meaning.

In the computational simulations of the model, form and meaning vectors are represented by 50 artificial (phonological and semantic) features, where only half of each feature set is significant. The model is trained on 50 and tested on three form-referent pairs. The simulation results show that the model can learn to correctly associate the form-meaning exemplars in the training set, and that learning becomes easier with more training data. In fact, the model demonstrates behaviour similar to fast mapping: in later stages, words are learned after only one or a few occurrences.

The analysis of the attention weights also shows patterns which suggest honing to the communicatively significant aspects of word form or meaning. Upon receiving enough exposure to the input exemplar pairs, the model successfully clusters form and meaning features into significant and insignificant groups (with negligible weights associated to the insignificant features). Thus the model can generalize word forms and meanings to new exemplars along the significant dimensions (e.g., voice or shape). Finally, the model can learn second labels for objects that are already associated with a word form, that is, despite mutual exclusivity.

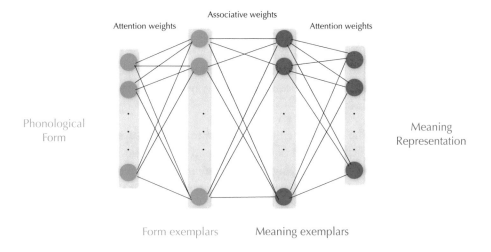

Associative weights

Attention weights   Attention weights

Phonological
Form

Meaning
Representation

Form exemplars   Meaning exemplars

Figure 3.1: The architecture of the associative word learning model of Regier (2005).

3.2.2   CASE STUDY: RULE-BASED CROSS-SITUATIONAL LEARNING

The computational model of Siskind (1996) was the first to investigate the feasibility of mapping words to their meaning representations via cross-situational learning, and in the presence of noise and referential uncertainty. Furthermore, many experimental findings on child word learning were replicated in this model. In many ways, it has been an influential model which shows the feasibility of learning words from sentential context, and accounting for many of the discussed phenomena in this domain using a single core learning mechanism.

Input to the model consists of a sequence of input utterances, where each utterance is paired with a number of meaning representations. This one-to-many pairing is supposed to simulate referential uncertainty: while hearing an utterance, different representations of its meaning can be hypothesized by the listener, only one of which can be correct. Meaning is represented as a logical expression, where the relations between predicate terms (e.g., verbs and adjectives) and their arguments (e.g., nouns, verb phrases) are shown as a (potentially nested) predicate structure. The meaning of each word is represented as two sets: one containing the meaning symbols that can possibly be part of the meaning of the word, and one containing symbols that are necessarily part of the word meaning. Learning in the model takes place via incremental application of a number of inference rules, which update sets of possible and necessary meaning symbols for each word in the current input utterance. A sample input item and the meaning representation of two sample words in this model are shown in Fig. 3.2.

The inference rules are expected to detect and apply cross-situational evidence from input, and refine word meanings accordingly. These rules integrate various assumptions and constraints into the model, some of which are mentioned below:

- *Composisionality*: the meaning of an utterance is derived from the meanings of its constituent words. As a result of applying this assumption, conceptual representations that include meaning symbols which are not part of the possible meaning sets of at least one word in the utterance are ruled out. Also, those conceptual representations which miss a necessary meaning symbol for any of the words in the utterance are left out.

- *Coverage*: only the meaning symbols that appear in the correct conceptual representation of an utterance can potentially be part of the meaning of a word in that utterance. Therefore by applying this rule, any meaning symbol that does not appear in the chosen utterance meaning will be omitted from the set of the possible meaning elements of all the words in that utterance.

- *Exclusivity*: each meaning symbol in the conceptual representation of the utterance can be part of the meaning of only one word in that utterance. Therefore, once a meaning symbol is part of the necessary meaning set of a word, it will be removed from the possible meaning sets of the rest of the words in the utterance.

Once a new input item is received, all the applicable rules are applied on it one by one, and the meaning representations of the words in the sentence are updated accordingly. The inference engine assumes an ideal input. Therefore, once the model encounters an 'imperfect' input item, it will update the meanings of the input words in a way that leads to incorrect representations. This is particularly problematic since the acquired word meanings are not revisable: once a meaning symbol is considered impossible for a word, it cannot be added back to the possible meaning set for that word. Similarly, once a meaning symbol is added to the necessary meaning symbols for a word, the model cannot remove it from that set in the future. However, an alternative mechanism is employed by Siskind's model for dealing with noise and homonymy. Whenever a potential inconsistency is detected as a result of processing a new input item (i.e., a word's necessary meaning symbols are not a subset of its possible meaning symbols), the model defines a new 'sense' for that word and starts to build its meaning from scratch. This mechanism allows the model to handle some degree of noise and to learn multiple meanings for the same word form, at the expense of creating many incorrect word senses which clutter the lexicon and affect the model's efficiency.

The model is evaluated on an artificially generated input, with controlled rates of referential uncertainty and noise. The computational simulation of the model displays a pattern similar to vocabulary spurt in children: learning is accelerated as the model is exposed to more input data, and the number of exposures needed for learning a word type is reduced over time. This shift from slow to fast word learning is a natural consequence of being exposed to more data, as opposed to a change in the underlying learning mechanism. Also, the model can learn second labels for familiar objects, but its homonymy-learning strategy (where a new sense is added to the lexical entry for a word whenever the model fails to maintain a consistent meaning representation for that word) does not explain the ease of learning homonymies with age.

A sample input item

John went to school.	⟷	GO(**John**,TO(**school**))
		MOVE(**John**,**feet**)
		WEAR(**John**,RED(**shirt**))

Meaning representation

words	Necessary meanings	Possible meanings
John	{**John**}	{**John**,**ball**}
took	{CAUSE}	{CAUSE,WANT,GO,TO,**arm**}

Figure 3.2: A sample input item and the meaning representation for two sample words in the word learning model of Siskind (1996).

3.2.3   CASE STUDY: PROBABILISTIC CROSS-SITUATIONAL LEARNING

Similar to Siskind (1996), the computational model of Fazly *et al.* (2010) focuses on learning the meaning of words from sentential context, and in the presence of noise and ambiguity. However, instead of incorporating a set of principles and constraints in a rule-based system, this model relies on a single probabilistic learning mechanism.

The input to the model consists of a sequence of pairs of an utterance and a corresponding scene representation. Compared to Siskind (1996), this model uses a rather naive representational framework for a scene: instead of a logical predicate structure, each scene is represented as a set of symbols representing the concepts or actions implied by the observed scene. The meaning of each word is defined as a probability distribution over all the meaning symbols, which the model incrementally builds over time as a result of processing input utterance-scene pairs one at a time.

Once presented with a new input item, the model calculates an alignment score for each word in the utterance and each meaning symbol in the scene. This alignment is calculated based on what the model knows about the meanings of words in the utterance up to this point in learning: the alignment score for a word and a meaning is proportional to the probabilistic association between the two (i.e., the probability of the meaning symbol given the word), and inversely proportional to the association between the meaning symbol and other words in the current utterance. Once the alignment score is calculated between all word-meaning pairs in the new input item, the meaning probabilities of the words in the utterance are updated accordingly. Words whose probability distribution is skewed towards the correct meaning element (i.e., the probability of the correct meaning symbol given the word exceeds a certain threshold) are considered *learned* by the model. A sample learning scenario is shown in Fig. 3.3.

The model is evaluated on a portion of CHILDES as follows: the child-directed utterances are extracted from CHILDES and fed to the model as input. However, the scene representation paired with each utterance is constructed artificially, by putting together a unique meaning symbol for each word type in the utterance. Referential uncertainty is simulated by merging the scene representations of each two adjacent utterances, and pairing that with the first utterance (thus the scene representation contains symbols which do not have a counterpart word in the utterance). In comparison to other models of word learning, a relatively large collection of data is used for evaluation (around 20, 000 input items, containing almost 2, 000 word types).

The results of the computational experiments show the same trend as those of Regier (2005) and Siskind (1996) in that learning becomes easier and more efficient as the model receives and processes more data. In the learning curve of the model across different simulations, a pattern similar to the vocabulary spurt in children can be observed, and the model needs fewer exposures for learning a word as it "ages". Moreover, a set of empirical findings related to fast mapping (mainly referent selection and retention) are simulated by the model. It is also shown that despite an initial reluctance, the model can learn synonymous and homonymous words, similar to what is observed in children.

The probabilistic nature of the model provides flexibility and robustness for the task of word learning, even in the presence of substantial noise and uncertainty in the input data. Also, many different behavioural patterns observed in children are accounted for using a simple, unified mechanism of word learning. However, the impoverished representation of form and meaning in this model does not allow for the investigation of other phenomena, such as honing of the meaning, or the tendency of children to assign labels to *basic* categories (e.g., Rosch *et al.*, 1976).

3.3   INTEGRATING OTHER INFORMATION RESOURCES

Most existing word learning models solely rely on the co-occurrence of words and referents. However, a number of models have attempted to enhance word learning by bringing other kinds of evidence into the process. We will review two groups of such models in the following sections: those which integrate syntactic information (such as the syntactic structure of a sentence or the syntactic categories of words) into a word learning model, and those which draw on social cues such as gaze, intonation or gesture to improve cross-situational word learning.

A few computational models have studied phenomena beyond learning a mapping between words and meanings. One example is the Bayesian model of Xu and Tenenbaum (2007), which focuses on how humans learn to generalize category meanings from examples of word usages. Assuming as prior knowledge a probabilistic version of the basic-level category bias (Rosch *et al.*, 1976; Markman, 1989), Xu and Tenenbaum's model learns appropriate category names for exemplar objects

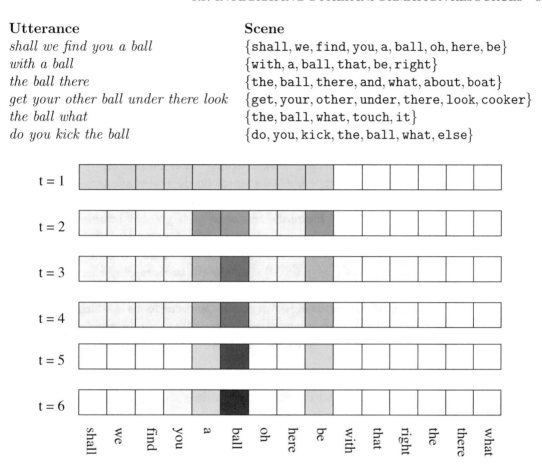

Figure 3.3: An example of a learning scenario in the model of Fazly *et al.* (2010): the meaning probability of the word *ball* changes through six exposures ($t = 1..6$).

by revising the prior bias through incorporating the statistical structure of the observed examples. Although their model shows similar behaviour to that of humans performing the same task, the model is tested only in a very specific word learning situation, and on a small sample of object exemplars.

3.3.1 SYNTACTIC STRUCTURE OF THE SENTENCE

A valuable source of information for mapping words to meanings is the syntactic structure of the sentence that a word appears in. There is substantial evidence that children are sensitive to the structural regularities of language from a very young age, and that they use these structural cues to find the referent of a novel word (e.g., Naigles and Hoff-Ginsberg, 1995; Gertner *et al.*, 2006), a hypothesis known as *syntactic bootstrapping* (Gleitman, 1990).

The syntactic bootstrapping account is in accordance with children's early sensitivity to distributional properties of language: one-year-old infants can recognize sentences from an artificial grammar after a short period of exposure (Gomez and Gerken, 1999), and 2-year-olds demonstrate robust knowledge of abstract lexical categories such as nouns, verbs and determiners (e.g., Gelman and Taylor, 1984; Kemp *et al.*, 2005). Therefore, it is likely that they draw on their knowledge of the structural regularities of language (and of lexical categories in particular) to facilitate word learning, especially in cases where cross-situational evidence is not reliable.

Despite the extensive body of experimental research on the role of syntactic knowledge in semantics acquisition, few computational models have been developed to explore the usefulness of lexical categories in learning word meanings. Maurits *et al.* (2009) has investigated the joint acquisition of word meaning and word order using a batch model. This model is tested on an artificial language with a simple relational structure of word meaning, and limited built-in possibilities for word order. The Bayesian model of Niyogi (2002) simulates the bootstrapping effects of syntactic and semantic knowledge in verb learning, i.e., the use of syntax to aid in inducing the semantics of a verb, and the use of semantics for narrowing down possible syntactic forms in which a verb can be expressed. However, this model relies on extensive prior knowledge about the associations between syntactic and semantic features, and it is tested on a toy language with very limited vocabulary and a constrained syntax.

Yu (2006) integrates information about syntactic categories of words into his model of cross-situational word learning, showing that this new source of information can improve the overall performance of the model. The model is evaluated on an experimental data set (collected by the author), where parents read and discuss story books with their children. The videos are manually annotated to identify the visible objects in the scene when each sentence is uttered. Yu's model builds on the batch algorithm of Yu (2005), augmented with a set of lexical categories automatically extracted from their data set using the grammar induction algorithm of Solan *et al.* (2005). The original cross-situational model is compared with an augmented version which takes into account the category membership of each word when estimating the association probabilities between words and referent objects. The original (cross-situational) model is compared against the augmented version based on the proportion of the correct lexical items (or word-meaning pairs), which the model learns after processing the data set, and their results suggest that integrating syntactic categories into the model enhances the performance.

Alishahi and Fazly (2010) present a probabilistic model of word learning which integrates cross-situational evidence and the knowledge of lexical categories into a single learning mechanism. This model is built on the probabilistic model of Fazly *et al.* (2008), augmented with the knowledge of the syntactic categories of words. It is assumed that an independent categorization module can process each sentence and determine the lexical category for each word based on its surrounding context. These categories are integrated into the base model as an alternative source of guidance for aligning words with appropriate semantic features in each scene. Computational simulations of the model show that using such information improves the performance in learning words.

3.3.2   SOCIAL CUES

Children are shown to be sensitive to social–pragmatic cues in the input, and they use them to map words to their meanings, especially at earlier stages of word learning (see, e.g., Hoff and Naigles, 2002, and the references therein). For example, Pan et al. (2005) show that non-verbal input such as pointing has a positive effect on children's vocabulary growth, and Butterworth (1991) shows that infants are sensitive to social cues such as monitoring and following gaze at a very young age. Moreover, analyzing child-directed speech shows that parents use specific vocal patterns when talking to children (such as higher pitch and pronounced intonation), which can serve as an attention-focusing device for highlighting focus words (Fernard, 1992).

Social and intentional cues such as gaze, prosody and pointing have been combined with cross-situational evidence in a number of computational models of word learning. For example, Yu and Ballard (2007) use video clips of mother-infant interactions from CHILDES, and manually label the visible objects when each utterance is uttered, as well as the objects of joint attention in each scene. Furthermore, they use low-level acoustic features in adult speech to spot the words that the speakers emphasize in each utterance. They propose an augmented version of an earlier model of cross-situational learning (Yu, 2005). In the extended model, the visual cues are used as weights for objects in each scene, and the prosodic cues are used as weights for words in each utterance. They show that integrating social cues improves the performance of a cross-situational model in most cases.

In a similar attempt, Frank et al. (2007) propose a Bayesian model of cross-situational word learning that can also learn which social cues are relevant for determining references of words, and can use them in mapping words to objects. They use the same video clips that Yu and Ballard (2007) use in their evaluations, but they mark additional social cues in their annotation (e.g., the infant's and mother's eyes and hands). They show that the Bayesian formulation of their model as well as the inclusion of a larger range of social cues yield a better coverage of the lexicon than the model of Yu and Ballard (2007). Moreover, using only domain-general probabilistic learning mechanisms, their model can explain various phenomena such as fast mapping and social generalization.

3.4   SUMMARY

Computational modeling of the process of word learning in children has been one of the more successful cases of using computational techniques in studying an aspect of human language acquisition. Several experimental studies hint at a change of behaviour in most children during the learning process (e.g., vocabulary spurt), and many conflicting proposals have been proposed to account for this pattern. However, many computational models have shown that most of these patterns can be a by-product of the statistical properties of the input that children receive. Most importantly, computational studies of word learning suggest that children's behaviour in this task is not necessarily due to a change in the underlying learning mechanism, or to the application of highly task-specific constraints or biases.

Despite the noteworthy findings of computational models of word learning, these models suffer from a lack of realistic semantic information which resembles the input data children receive. Moreover, the study of word learning by these models is generally limited to the simple mappings between nouns and concrete objects, and the relational or abstract meaning representations are often ignored. Also, unlike the linguistic theories of word learning such as syntactic bootstrapping or embodied cognition, computational studies of word learning have mostly been carried in isolation and independently of the other aspects of language acquisition.

CHAPTER 4

Putting Words Together

Natural languages have a complex structure. Word forms change systematically in different usages, such as different tenses of verbs or singular versus plural forms of nouns. The syntactic behaviour of words is mainly determined by the lexical categories that they belong to: most of the nouns, prepositions and verbs in each language follow the same patterns of combination with other words in a sentential context. Furthermore, the structure of natural language sentences follows highly regular patterns.

Acquisition of inflectional morphology, which determines the regularities governing word forms has been studied for a long time and from different view points. The common view advocated by generative linguists assumes that humans possess and use abstract knowledge of the regularities that govern form from the beginning, where such knowledge is represented as a rule-based system. An alternative view assumes that an analogy-based mechanism is at play when generating new word forms. Section 4.1 reviews different accounts of learning morphology and the computational trends for studying this process. We will discuss the acquisition of English past tense in more detail since it has been extensively investigated through several experimental and computational studies.

Section 4.2 focuses on the induction of lexical categories from input. Categories such as nouns, verbs, prepositions and auxiliaries are the essential building blocks of adult grammar. They constitute the elements that are combined and ordered to produce and understand the infinite number of sentences possible in any language. Development of the ability to assign words to their appropriate syntactic categories is therefore crucial to language acquisition. We will review existing computational models of learning categories from text, and the evaluation techniques used for assessing these models.

Learning the syntactic structure of language has been considered as the core challenge of learning a language. Section 4.3 looks at different theoretical and computational approaches to the study of syntax. Nativist and usage-based accounts of language acquisition are reviewed and their computational simulations are discussed. From each group, we examine a few representative case studies to demonstrate the diverse modeling approaches and frameworks used for tackling the problem of learning structural properties of language from text.

4.1 MORPHOLOGY: WORD FORM REGULARITIES

The inflectional formation of words (such as verb tenses or plural noun forms) follows highly regular patterns in most natural languages. However, in each language there are also many words which do not follow these general regularities and demonstrate an idiosyncratic behaviour. In the domain of inflectional morphology, it has been widely debated whether the formation of regular patterns is due to a rule-based or an analogy-based process. Generative linguistics states that humans possess a collection of abstract rules which they apply to word forms. However, many argue that new forms are produced based on their surface (i.e., phonological) similarity to previously seen forms.

The developmental course of learning morphology in children shows a rather consistent pattern, often known as a *U-shaped learning curve*: Early on, many children correctly produce a small set of inflected forms. This conservative phase is followed by a generalization phase, where children seem to have grasped the general regularities governing form and apply them to new or familiar instances. This process sometimes leads to overgeneralization, where a default pattern is applied to an irregular form (e.g., *womans* or *goed*). However, children eventually recover from making overgeneralization mistakes, and converge to adult-level performance.

4.1.1   COMPUTATIONAL MODELS OF LEARNING MORPHOLOGY

In computational linguistics, several machine learning algorithms have been proposed for supervised and unsupervised learning of the morphological regularities and idiosyncrasies of language (Roark and Sproat, 2007). Supervised algorithms often rely on a training set which consists of a list of words, each annotated with its inflected forms (e.g., Stroppa and Yvon, 2005; Wicentowski and Yarowsky, 2003; Chrupała *et al.*, 2008; Toutanova and Cherry, 2009). Unsupervised methods use machine learning and pattern recognition algorithms to extract widespread inflectional patterns from a corpus (e.g., Goldsmith, 2001; Schone and Jurafsky, 2001; Neuvel and Fulop, 2002). However, these models are not concerned with replicating and explaining the specific learning trajectories observed in children, such as the U-shaped learning curve described in the previous section.

In the domain of cognitive modeling, the acquisition of morphology has been mostly studied on a limited set of cases, such as English past tense and German plural form (Prasada and Pinker, 1993; Rumelhart and McClelland, 1987; Plunkett and Marchman, 1991; Nakisia *et al.*, 2000; Hahn and Nakisa, 2000). The agenda behind these models is to evaluate the competence of rule-based, analogy-based and associative mechanisms of learning morphology. These approaches have been compared against each other based on their learning capacity, flexibility in handling regular versus irregular forms, and their descriptive power in accounting for the overgeneralization patterns that are found in the experimental data. We will next look more closely at these modeling approaches for studying the acquisition of past tense verbs in English.

4.1.2   CASE STUDY: LEARNING ENGLISH PAST TENSE

The acquisition of past tense in English has been treated by many cognitive scientists as the ultimate case study for development of morphology in children. Past tense in English follows a relatively simple pattern: the majority of verbs in the language are formed by adding the suffix '-ed' to the stem of the verb. However, most of the highly frequent verbs have an irregular past tense form. Some of these irregular forms are not systematically related to the stem form (i.e., *go* → *went*), whereas others demonstrate less common but systematic patterns (e.g., unchanged stem form such as *put* and *hit*, or a vowel change such as *sing* and *drink*). Empirical findings and extensive analysis of child-produced language shows a pronounced version of the U-shaped learning curve for past tense verbs in English (Marcus *et al.*, 1992). Early on, children correctly produce a small set of both regular and irregular forms, followed by an overgeneralization period where the dominant pattern is applied to an irregular form (e.g., *he eated the cake*). Such mistakes diminish over time.

Following these findings, two different approaches were taken for explaining the behaviour of children. The "dual-route" architecture (e.g., Pinker, 1991; Prasada and Pinker, 1993) states that regular and irregular past tense forms are produced via two qualitatively different mechanisms (or routes): whereas a general, default rule (or a small set of such rules) is used for processing the regular verbs, the irregular forms must be fetched from memory through an associative mechanism. According to this theory, overgeneralization happens when a rule is applied to an irregular stem form by mistake (e.g., due to the yet weak association between the verb stem and its past tense form). After sufficient exposure to the irregular form, the association becomes entrenched and 'blocks' the application of the rule(s), which prevents the production of an overgeneralization error. The architecture of the dual-route model is shown in Fig. 4.1. This architecture is computationally implemented in a number of models, most notably in Taatgen and Anderson (2002), a hybrid ACT-R model that shows U-shaped learning without direct feedback.

Alternatively, many have argued that a single connectionist network can learn and produce both regular and irregular forms through a single associative mechanism (e.g., Rumelhart and McClelland, 1987; Plunkett and Marchman, 1991; Daugherty and Seidenberg, 1992, see Christiansen and Chater (1999) for an overview). Most of these models use a feed-forward connectionist network, where the input and output layers represent the stem and the inflected form as arrays of phonological features. Early in training these models show a tendency to overgeneralize, but by the end of training they exhibit near-perfect performance. The U-shaped performance is achieved using a single learning mechanism, however in most cases the onset of overgeneralization and recovery highly depends on the training regime (e.g., sudden change in the size of the vocabulary in the training set).

4.2   FORMATION OF LEXICAL CATEGORIES

Psycholinguistic studies suggest that early on children acquire robust knowledge of some of the abstract lexical categories such as nouns and determiners. For example, Gelman and Taylor (1984) show that two-year-olds treat novel words which do not follow a determiner (e.g., *Look! This is Zag!*) as a proper name which refers to an individual. In contrast, they tend to interpret novel words which do follow a determiner (e.g., *Look! This is a zag!*) as a mass noun. However, learning lexical categories takes place gradually, and not all categories are learned at the same time. For example, Tomasello *et al.* (1997) show that two-year-olds are more productive with nouns than with verbs, in that they use novel nouns more frequently and in more diverse contexts. Similarly, Kemp *et al.* (2005) show that children's tendency to combine novel nouns with various determiners or adjectives differs with age, and these categories are slowly formed over the years.

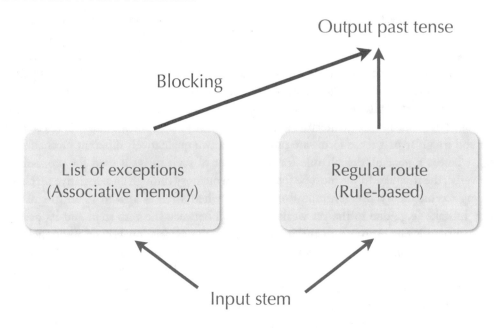

Figure 4.1: The architecture of the dual-route model of English past tense (Pinker, 1991).

How children gain knowledge of syntactic categories is an open question. Children's grouping of words into categories might be based on various cues, including the phonological and morphological properties of a word, distributional information about its surrounding context, and its semantic features. Shi *et al.* (1999) report that very young infants can discriminate between two lists of English content and function words based only on perceptual (surface) cues. Mintz (2002) argues that bigram regularity cannot explain categorization in artificial grammar experiments. However, their experimental findings show that adults can categorize words in an artificial language based on their occurrence within frames (or the preceding and following words). Moreover, Mintz (2003) analyzes child-directed speech, and argues that frequent frames found in these data are a reliable information unit for the formation of accurate categories.

The distributional properties of the local context of a word have been extensively studied, and used in various computational models of category induction. However, the unsupervised nature of these models makes their assessment a challenge (since there is no gold-standard to compare the output of the model against), and the evaluation techniques proposed in the literature are limited. In the following sections, we will review existing computational models of lexical category induction and the evaluation methodologies used for assessing them.

4.2.1   COMPUTATIONAL MODELS OF LEXICAL CATEGORY INDUCTION

Several machine learning techniques have used distributional information for categorizing words from large text corpora (e.g., Brown *et al.*, 1992; Schütze, 1993; Clark, 2000). These models often use iterative, unsupervised methods that partition the vocabulary into a set of optimum clusters. The generated clusters are intuitive, and can be used in different tasks such as word prediction and parsing. Although many such models do not aim at studying human category induction, they confirm the learnability of abstract word categories, and show that distributional cues are a useful source of information for this purpose.

The model of Redington *et al.* (1998) specifically investigates the problem of inducing lexical categories from child-directed data. A small set of target and context words are chosen based on their frequency in CHILDES, and each target word is represented as a context vector. A hierarchical clustering algorithm is applied to the target words, and the final hierarchy is cut at an intuitive level. This procedure results in a number of disconnected clusters, which are compared to a set of gold-standard categories (noun, verb, etc.) in which each word belongs to only one category. Several analyses are conducted on the final set of clusters to study the effect of various factors in the quality of clustering. For example, it is shown that the closer the context position to the target word, the more information it carries about the syntactic category of the target. Also, preceding context appears to be more useful than the succeeding context. However, including a larger number of context words (i.e., the size of the context vector) does not improve the quality of the learned clusters.

The process of learning lexical categories by children is necessarily incremental. Human language acquisition is bounded by memory and processing limitations, and it is implausible that humans process large volumes of text at once and induce an optimum set of categories. However, most of the existing models of lexical category induction rely on iterative processing of the whole corpus. There have only been a few previous attempts at applying an incremental method to category acquisition. The model of Cartwright and Brent (1997) uses an algorithm which incrementally forms word clusters: each word in an input sentence is assigned a new label, and the sentence is represented as a template for these labels. Word clusters are gradually merged so that a Minimum Description Length criterion for a template grammar is optimized. The model successfully learns proper lexical categories on artificially generated language, and generalizes to some extent to natural language. However, treating the whole sentence as a contextual unit sacrifices a degree of incrementality, and makes the model less robust to noise in the input.

The model of Parisien *et al.* (2008) uses a Bayesian clustering algorithm that can cope with ambiguity, and exhibits the developmental trends observed in children (e.g., the order of acquisition of different categories). The model incorporates an initial word-based bias when forming categories (different word types are put into different categories). This bias makes the model overly sensitive to context diversity, and results in the creation of sparse clusters. To overcome the problem, a boot-strapping component is introduced which estimates the likelihood of a new word usage belonging to a cluster based on the *categories* (instead of the words) preceding the target word. Also, a periodical cluster reorganization mechanism is introduced. These extensions improve the overall performance of the model, given that the model receives a substantial amount of training data. In a similar approach, Chrupała and Alishahi (2010) use an incremental, entropy-based algorithm for clustering words based on their context. Their model is more efficient in forming informative categories from smaller data sets, but does not implement a reorganization mechanism for revising the previous categorization decisions.

4.2.2   EVALUATION OF THE INDUCED CATEGORIES

There is no standard and straightforward method for evaluating unsupervised models of category learning (see Clark, 2003, for discussion). Many unsupervised models of lexical category acquisition treat the traditional part of speech (PoS) tags as the gold standard, and measure the accuracy and completeness of their induced categories based on how closely they resemble the PoS categories (e.g., Redington *et al.*, 1998; Mintz, 2003; Parisien *et al.*, 2008). However, it is not at all clear whether humans form the same type of categories. In fact, many language tasks might benefit from finer-grained categories than the traditional PoS tags used for corpus annotation.

Frank *et al.* (2009) propose a different, automatically generated set of gold standard categories for evaluating an unsupervised categorization model. The gold-standard categories are formed according to the concept of "substitutability": if one word can be replaced by another and the resulting sentence is still grammatical, then there is a good chance that the two words belong to the same category. Three-word frames are extracted from the training data, and used to form the gold standard categories based on the words that appear in the same frame. The authors emphasize that in order to provide some degree of generalization, it is important to use different data sets for forming the gold-standard categories and performing the evaluation. However, the resulting categories are bound to be incomplete, and using them as gold standard inevitably favors categorization models which use a similar frame-based principle.

All in all, using any set of gold-standard categories for evaluating an unsupervised categorization model has the disadvantage of favoring one set of principles and intuitions over another; that is, assuming that there is a *correct* set of categories which the model should converge to. Alternatively, automatically induced categories can be evaluated based on how *useful* they are in performing different tasks. Such a usage-based approach is taken by Clark (2000), where the perplexity of a finite-state model is used to compare different category sets. Chrupała and Alishahi (2010) extend this idea by emphasizing that the ultimate goal of a category induction model is to form categories that can be efficiently used in a variety of language tasks. They propose a number of tasks for which they compare the performance based on various category sets, including word prediction, grammaticality judgment and inferring semantic properties of a novel word based on the surrounding context.

4.3   LEARNING STRUCTURAL KNOWLEDGE OF LANGUAGE

Children produce their first recognizable words around 12–18 months of age. They start combining words together and produce their first phrases around the age of two, and shortly after produce more complex utterances. Between age one and six, children acquire extensive skills in using language, and by ten to twelve years of age they have reached adult-level competence in using complex constructions and a large lexicon (Clark, 2009).

In formal studies of language learnability, the availability of corrective feedback (i.e., information about which strings of words do not belong to a language), or *direct negative evidence*, plays an important role (a point we will get back to later in this section). The (grammatical) linguistic input that a child receives from its environment is referred to as *positive evidence*. Some studies suggest that there is no reliable corrective feedback available to children, and even if such feedback is provided, children ignore it (McNeill, 1966; Brown and Hanlon, 1970; Marcus, 1993). Others suggest that substantial amount of negative evidence can be found in child-directed speech, and this data may play an important role in the learning process (Saxton, 2000; Chouinard and Clark, 2003). However, it is safe to assume that not every child is consistently corrected for every error that they make, and learning a language must be possible only by receiving and processing more input from the environment.

The acquisition of the syntactic structure of language, or how children learn to put words together and build well-formed sentences, has been the subject of much debate among linguists and psychologists. One of the most influential (and more recently, controversial) theories in this domain was proposed by Chomsky (1986), who claimed that children are equipped with a domain specific and innate representation of the structure of language. This theory is often referred to as the nativist account of language.

4.3.1   NATIVIST ACCOUNTS OF SYNTAX

In the nativist account knowing a language involves knowing a grammar, a language-specific formalism for producing and interpreting well-formed word sequences (or sentences). The task of learning a language is defined as identifying the correct grammar. In this view, the child has to converge on the knowledge structures that constitute the grammar, or find the target grammar in a hypothesis-space of candidate grammars, based on linguistic experience (Chomsky, 1965).

The principal argument for linguistic nativism is that the input data that children have access to (*Primary Linguistic Data*, or PLD) is not sufficiently rich for them to learn the grammar of the language. This argument is known as the *Argument from the Poverty of Stimulus* (or APS). Drawing on early formal studies of language learnability (which we will briefly review in Section 4.3.2), the advocates of linguistic nativism suggest that learning a language is not possible unless the space of hypothesized grammars is severely constrained by innate prior knowledge about the properties of the grammar. More specifically, Chomsky (1981) proposed that infants must be born with a Universal Grammar (UG), an innate specification of the syntactic structure of natural languages. According to this proposal, the grammatical knowledge of language is represented by a finite set of fundamental principles that are common to all languages, and a finite set of parameters that determine syntactic variability amongst languages. This framework is often referred to as *Principles and Parameters* (or P & P). The view that children are born with knowledge of Universal Grammar assumes that all natural languages have a common structural basis, and is in line with findings of the behavioural studies indicating that various types of knowledge are present in children as young as they can be tested.

The nativist view of language is mainly concerned with the characterization of the knowledge of an idealized speaker of the language, or her *competence*. In other words, competence determines what it means to "know" a language. On the other hand, the *performance* of the language user indicates how the knowledge of language is used in various tasks such as language comprehension and production. The nativist account often attributes children's learning trajectory and grammatical mistakes to performance issues such as memory and processing constraints and computational load, and does not take empirical findings on child language acquisition into consideration when studying the properties of UG. This view implies a *continuity assumption*: children are assumed to have the same competence (i.e., the same representation of syntactic rules and categories) as adults.

4.3.2 FORMAL STUDIES OF LEARNABILITY

The argument from the poverty of stimulus was partly motivated by the mathematical work of Gold (1967), which indicated that learners cannot converge on the correct grammar from an infinitely large corpus without having access to substantial negative evidence. In one of the first formal models of learnability, Gold (1967) proposed a framework for characterizing language learnability as convergence to a grammar from exposure to an infinite sequence of linguistic data. Various extensions to this framework have been proposed for refining the original model of Gold (e.g., Jain, 1999; De La Higuera, 1997).

As a solution to Gold's "no negative evidence" problem, subsequent research draws on probability theory to infer "indirect negative evidence" (INF) from linguistic data, and to argue that the distributional properties of input compensates for the absence of negative data (Angluin, 1988; Clark and Lappin, 2010a). Moreover, Horning (1972) proved that using a proper sample of linguistic data, phrase-structure grammars are learnable with high probability within a statistical tolerance. As opposed to the original approach to language learnability which aims at finding the correct grammar, the probabilistic approach to learnability attempts to learn the correct *distribution* over strings that the grammar produces. Later extensions of Horning's approach generalize the original findings to a broad range of distributions (see Clark and Lappin (2010a) for a thorough discussion).

The best known theory of probabilistic learning, the Probably Approximately Correct (PAC) model (Valiant, 1984) improves significantly on the Gold model in that it offers a more plausible treatment of convergence, but it is not suitable for studying child language acquisition since it requires input data that is labelled for grammaticality. However, modifications of this paradigm have been proposed which remove labels from input data, and improve learnability by restricting the class of distributions (e.g., Clark and Lappin, 2010a). That said, most formal models of learnability focus on investigating which classes of languages can be learned from finite or infinite data, without being concerned about the efficiency of learning.

4.3.3   CASE STUDY: MODELS OF P & P

According to the Principles and Parameters framework, the learner is provided with innate knowledge of a parametrized grammar, or the distinctive properties which identify natural language grammars. For example, a binary parameter can determine whether or not the subject of a sentence must be overtly pronounced in a particular language. Therefore, the learning process is defined as finding the correct values for these N parameters based on exposure to linguistic data. In other words, the correct grammar has to be found in a search space of size 2^N. It has been suggested that 30–40 parameters are needed for representing points of variation between languages (Clark, 1992; Kayne, 2000), in which case, UG is describing a hypothesis space of over a billion grammars.

A number of algorithms for learning a grammar have been proposed within the P & P framework (Gibson and Wexler, 1994; Wacholder, 1995; Fodor, 1998; Sakas and Fodor, 2001; Yang, 2002; Buttery, 2006). Most of these algorithms have the same structure: they analyze each input string in turn, and set the parameter values accordingly, thus systematically moving from one grammar to the next within the hypothesis space. The learner can set a parameter upon receiving evidence from an example of linguistic input which exhibits that parameter. Such examples are called *triggers*. However, very often language examples contain ambiguous evidence for the properties that the learner is looking for. One approach to dealing with ambiguous triggers is to choose one of the possible interpretations and set the parameter values according to that interpretation. Alternatively, the learner can ignore the trigger and wait for an unambiguous one.

The Triggering Learning Algorithm (TLA) of Gibson and Wexler (1994) adopts the first approach: it analyzes incoming triggers using the current settings for a set of binary parameters, and modifies their values if they conflict with the properties of the incoming triggers. The TLA is error-driven; that is, it randomly modifies a parameter value every time the learner cannot parse the current input. This greedy approach accelerates learning but has a few problems: the learner might be caught in local maxima or never converge to the correct grammar. Also, the algorithm cannot distinguish between grammatical and erroneous sentences, and will incorrectly set the parameter values when facing a noisy input.

The model of Structural Triggers Learner (STL) of Fodor (1998) takes a conservative approach to processing triggers: it carries out a structural analysis of the input examples, and ignores the ambiguous ones entirely. This method avoids converging on the wrong grammar but is wasteful of the language examples it receives. The parameters in this model are not binary variables, but subtrees (or treelets) which construct the UG. The algorithm allows several treelets to be learnt during a single parse, which enhances the learning speed. However, the wait for an unambiguous parse to learn from might be very long. Similar to the TLS, the STL cannot handle noisy input. The parameter setting model of Dresher and Kaye (1990) suggests an alternative approach to processing ambiguous triggers by placing a careful ordering on the properties, which allows for choosing the correct interpretation to use for the ambiguous trigger.

The Variational Learner of Yang (2002) incorporates a statistical approach for dealing with this problem. In this model, each parameter in a candidate grammar is associated with a weight. Upon receiving a trigger, the parameter weights in the selected grammar are either rewarded or penalized depending on whether or not the grammar can parse the trigger. Acquisition is complete when the grammar weights become approximately constant. However, a problem with this model is that it does not reward or punish the parameters individually. Instead, when a grammar successfully parses a trigger, all of its parameters are rewarded. The Variational Learner model has been shown to be capable of making quantitative predictions over developmental language patterns.

Despite ongoing research on learning algorithms in the P & P framework, there are no implemented models that can demonstrate the learnability of a grammar from realistic linguistic input for a reasonable subset of languages. In addition to the computational challenges of implementing the principles and parameters framework such as the huge search space and local maxima, the cognitive plausibility of such implementations has also been questioned. Revisiting and resetting the parameter values after processing each input trigger implies that the learner constantly jumps from one grammar to another, as opposed to gradually develop a structural knowledge of the language.

4.3.4   USAGE-BASED ACCOUNTS OF SYNTAX

The nativist tradition of assuming continuity between child and adult language has been challenged by a number of recent empirical findings about child language learning. Studies using transcripts of real language usage have shown that children's speech for at least the first two years of age is remarkably restricted: certain constructions are produced with only a small set of frequent verbs, and a large number of utterances are built from lexically specific frames (Tomasello, 2000; Lieven *et al.*, 2003). Many experimental studies on children also support this view (e.g., Olguin and Tomasello, 1993; Akhtar, 1999).

These findings suggest an alternative, *usage-based* account of language learning in which children learn abstract regularities and constructions of language from input alone, without guidance in the form of innate principles (e.g., MacWhinney, 1987; Tomasello, 2003). The usage-based account claims that a child's progress to linguistic productivity is gradual, starting with knowledge of specific items and restricted abstractions rather than general categories and rules. One such important theory is the *Verb Island Hypothesis* of Tomasello (2003), which states that children have an early period in which each verb they learn forms its own "island" consisting of verb-specific constructions with open nominal slots. Children use cognitive and socio-cognitive processes such as imitation (reproducing the language adults produce for the same communicative function), analogy, and structure mapping (detecting both structural and functional similarities in utterances independent of the specific words involved) to gradually categorize the relational-syntactic structure of their various item-based constructions, and therefore become productive with their language in more adult-like ways.

Although the evidence supporting this view is strong, it tends to be limited to a construction here or an utterance frame there. Wide-coverage models must be developed that can account for the usage-based acquisition of language from child-directed speech. There have been two different approaches to modeling usage-based acquisition of syntactic structure from input data. One approach, inspired by the connectionist models of language, takes a 'revisionist' perspective on the strict symbolic rules thought to underlie language. It proposes a distributed representation of linguistic knowledge as an alternative to formal grammars. We will look at an example of this view in the next section.

A second approach is motivated by a renewed interest in linguistics in the stochastic properties of language, and recent psycholinguistic findings which suggest that children are sensitive to statistical cues in the input at a very young age (e.g., Saffran *et al.*, 1996; Thompson and Newport, 2007). Following this perspective, various statistical machine learning techniques have been employed to induce a grammar from textual input. We will review these models in Section 4.3.6, and look at a case study in Section 4.3.7.

4.3.5   CASE STUDY: DISTRIBUTIONAL REPRESENTATION OF SYNTACTIC STRUCTURE

Inspired by the development of connectionism, an alternative view of syntax emerged. According to this view learning the structural properties of a language is not equated with knowing a grammar. Instead, knowledge of language is something that develops in the course of learning to communicate through comprehension and production. In a connectionist model of language learning and use, knowledge of language is represented by the distributed activation patterns of the nodes in a network, determined by the weights on the connections between nodes. Learning in turn consists of changing these weights in order to improve the performance of a particular task that the model is trained for (e.g., word production or assigning meaning to sentences). In other words, learning aims to reduce the discrepancy between actual and desired output patterns of activation.

Several connectionist models of language learning have been developed to demonstrate that abstract linguistic structures can emerge from enough exposure to instances of language usage. Most of these models are trained on pairings of a sentence and its semantic interpretation, for example in terms of the semantic properties of verbs and the thematic roles of the arguments (McClelland and Kawamoto, 1986; Allen, 1997; Allen and Seidenberg, 1999; Desai, 2002). We will discuss these models in detail in Chapter 5.

The influential model of Elman (1990, 1991), however, attempts to learn syntactic structure from sequences of words. It introduces Simple Recurrent Networks (SRN) as an extended version of a standard feed-forward neural network with an additional *context layer*. The context layer always keeps a copy of the hidden layer activations from the previous time step, and feeds it back to the model as (part of) the input vector (Fig. 4.2 demonstrates this architecture). That way, the model can make decisions based on what it has seen before, or the context of each word. The model is trained to predict the next input word, for sentences generated by a small context-free grammar.

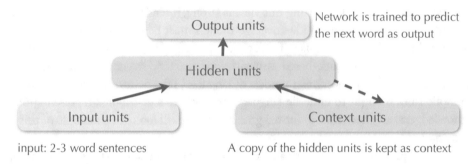

Figure 4.2: The architecture of the SRN network used in the model of Elman (1991).

In Elman (1990), words are chosen from thirteen classes of nouns and verbs, and encoded by a vector in which each word is represented by a different bit, i.e. exactly one dimension is set to one and while the rest are zero. This encoding scheme guarantees that vectors reflect nothing about the form class or meaning of the words. The task given to the network is to learn to predict the order of successive words. The network is trained on a sequence of vectors representing an input sequence, where each word in the sequence is fed to the model one at a time. The network learns an abstract representation of grammatical relations through learning lexical categories of the input words such as nouns and verbs (with further subcategorization of nouns as animate/inanimate, human/non-human, etc.), and the permitted combination of these categories in a sentence.

Elman (1991) extends the previous model by using stimuli in which there are underlying hierarchical and recursive relationships (e.g., subject nouns agree with their verbs; verbs have different argument structures; recursive relative clauses are permitted). Also, an end-of-sentence marker is introduced which can potentially occur anywhere in a string where a grammatical sentence might be terminated. An analysis of the hidden unit activation patterns shows that the network develops distributed representations which encode the relevant grammatical relations and hierarchical constituent structure. Elman's model is an important demonstration of the possibility of categorizing and learning abstract structures from strings of words.

Distributional models of syntax have appealing properties. They use a single mechanism for the learning and use of language. These models have a highly probabilistic nature, and are capable of deriving structural regularities from noisy or variable input. Moreover, the statistical aspects of the input can be naturally encoded into the linguistic knowledge. However, these models are not easily scalable to larger vocabularies or grammars, and are generally very sensitive to the training environment (but see Collobert and Weston (2008)).

4.3.6   GRAMMAR INDUCTION FROM CORPORA

The nativist assumption that knowledge of language is internally represented by abstract linguistic rules shifted the focus of computational studies to search for an optimal formal grammar, and ignore the stochastic aspects of language (Chater and Manning, 2006).[1] However, in natural language processing (NLP), the practical challenge of parsing and interpreting large text corpora has led to a strong focus on probabilistic methods and statistical machine learning techniques. Although most of the mainstream NLP systems pursue a more applied goal (processing text corpora in order to perform a particular task with high accuracy), their success in extracting various aspects of syntactic knowledge from large bodies of text provides a valuable source of ideas and hypotheses for cognitive models of language.

Many computational systems have been developed for grammar induction from corpora (e.g., Adriaans, 1992, 2001; Stolcke and Omohundro, 1994; van Zaanen, 2000; Clark, 2001, 2006; Pereira, 2000; Klein and Manning, 2002; Solan et al., 2004; Lappin and Shieber, 2007, see Chater and Manning (2006) and Clark and Lappin (2010b) for an overview). In these models, the space of possible grammars that can be generated from the input data is defined, and a learning algorithm is trained on (sometimes a part-of-speech-tagged version of) the input corpus to find the best grammar that assigns syntactic structures to unseen data. The quality of the grammar is usually compared against a gold-standard parsed data set, based on the accurate recognition of the constituent boundaries. These models are not cognitively motivated, and their success in acquiring accurate approximations of human grammatical knowledge does not show that humans learn in a similar way (in fact many of them explicitly state that their approach is not meant as a model of human language acquisition, e.g., Clark (2001) and Klein and Manning (2002)). Nevertheless, they suggest that grammar induction from linguistic evidence of the kind available to children is feasible via domain general learning techniques.

A few computational models have been developed which focus on the cognitive aspects of learning a grammar, and they attempt to provide explanations for empirical findings on human grammar learning. One such example is the Model of Syntax Acquisition in Children (MOSAIC; Jones et al., 2000; Gobet et al., 2004)). This model constructs a hierarchical network from an input corpus of child-directed speech, which can in turn be used to produce new utterances that simulate child production data. The model has been shown to simulate a number of empirical findings regarding early language acquisition in several languages. We will look more closely at this model in the next section.

Another cognitive model of syntax acquisition is the model of Bannard et al. (2009). This model induces a lexically specific context free grammar (where each rule contains some specific word or words) from input corpora of transcriptions of child-produced speech. A Bayesian procedure is used for choosing the best fitting grammar from each input corpus, where smaller and more lexicalized grammars have a higher prior probability. They analyze the grammars learned for children of different age groups, and show that at two years of age the grammars allow for limited productivity and generalizability. However, grammars extracted from the speech of three year-olds show increased productivity and favour more abstract categories. In a similar vein, Perfors et al. (2006)

---

[1] Similarly in language processing, it was assumed that disambiguation occurs using *structural* features of the trees, and is not guided by the frequency of usage of different word combinations or constructions (e.g., Frazier and Fodor, 1978; Frazier, 1979).

present a model of Bayesian inference which selects the appropriate grammar for auxiliary fronting rule from child-directed data. The hypothesis space contains flat grammars (a list of sentences), probabilistic regular grammars and probabilistic context-free grammars. The prior probability of each grammar is determined based on its complexity (i.e., the number of vocabulary items, non-terminals and productions used in its definition). Their experimental results show a transition from highly lexicalized grammars to more abstract ones as the model/child receives more input, a trend that is in line with the item-based account of language acquisition.

A different approach follows the Data-Oriented Parsing paradigm (DOP; Bod, 1992) for simulating grammar acquisition. DOP is a model of supervised parsing, which estimates the likelihood of all possible structures given in an annotated input corpus, and uses these probabilities in building a structural description for a new utterance. Bod (2009) proposes an unsupervised version of this model. The extended version extracts all possible unlabeled binary trees from an unannotated training set and estimates their probabilities, which it uses to determine the most likely tree for an utterance. Borensztajn et al. (2009) use DOP for investigating the most probable constituents (or multi-word units) in child-produced data, and they show a progression from very concrete towards abstract constructions.

Onnis et al. (2002) use minimum description length to investigate a simplicity bias in recovering from overgeneralization, i.e., that cognitive systems seek the hypothesis that provides the briefest representation of the available data. They formulate the problem as choosing the candidate model of the right complexity to describe the corpus data, as determined by the simplicity principle. They show that a grammatical representation that incorporates both general rules and lexical exceptions provides a simpler encoding as the learner is exposed to larger amounts of data. While this model does not simulate the acquisition of a grammar (it compares pre-specified hypotheses instead), this work lends support to the assumption that verb-specific knowledge must be combined with that of general constructions for effective learning.

4.3.7   CASE STUDY: MOSAIC

MOSAIC (Model Of Syntax Acquisition In Children) (Jones et al., 2000; Gobet et al., 2004) is a computational model that learns from raw text, and it produces utterances similar to those children produce. MOSAIC analyzes the distributional characteristics present in the input using two discrimination- and generalization-based learning mechanisms. The first mechanism grows an n-ary discrimination network consisting of nodes connected by directed test links, where each node encodes a single word and each test link encodes the difference between the contents of the connected nodes. The second mechanism creates a new type of connection, a *generative link*, between two nodes which share a certain percentage of words surrounding them. The model generates output by traversing the network and outputting the contents of the visited links. Fig. 4.3 shows a snapshot of an induced discrimination network by this model.

The use of generative links enables the model to demonstrate limited generalization abilities. MOSAIC was trained on a subset of CHILDES, and used to simulate a number of phenomena

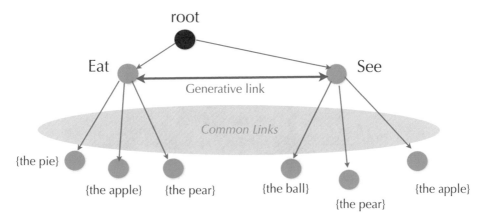

Figure 4.3: A sample portion of a discrimination network learned by MOSAIC (Jones *et al.*, 2000).

in language acquisition, including the verb island phenomenon (Jones *et al.*, 2000), the optional infinitive phenomenon in English (Gobet *et al.*, 2004) and Dutch (Freudenthal *et al.*, 2006), subject omission (Freudenthal *et al.*, 2007) and referential properties of root infinitives in Dutch, German and English (Freudenthal *et al.*, 2009). However, the lack of semantic knowledge prevents the model from performing any meaningful generalization, and the generalized sentences are limited to the high-frequency terms.

4.4   SUMMARY

Early computational models were mostly implementations of the Principles and Parameters proposal, and their goal was to find a set of parameters which can reflect the diversity of natural languages but still limit the extent of the hypothesis space. However, finding the right set of parameters and developing an efficient learning algorithm which can converge to the correct grammar proved to be a challenge. The connectionist models suggested alternative representations of the structural knowledge of language, and they showed that abstract properties of language can emerge from instances of usage. But these models were limited in the scale and complexity of the syntactic constructions that they could learn.

Recent advances in statistical methods of grammar induction from text corpora have allowed for the development of more sophisticated models of syntax acquisition from large collections of data. The range of constructions that are learned by these models are still more limited in variety and complexity compared to those of interest to linguistic theories. However, the underlying statistical techniques and probabilistic representations provide a flexible and robust framework for language learning, and they naturally incorporate the role of linguistic experience in language processing.

CHAPTER 5

Form–Meaning Associations

The relational meaning of a sentence is determined not only by the meaning of each of its words, but also by its syntactic structure: *Pat hit Matt* carries a very different meaning than *Matt hit Pat*. The representation and acquisition of syntax have been historically studied in isolation and independently of the inherent associations between the sentential form and its relational meaning. As mentioned in the previous chapter, much attention has been paid to the well-formedness of a sentence in a language according to a formal, context-free representation of the linguistic structure (or the grammar). However, words are put together to convey a message, and the acceptability of a sentence is highly influenced by the semantic properties of the predicate terms in language (verbs, adjectives, preposition etc.) and the arguments that they take.

Children are aware of the systematic form-meaning associations in language, and they use them to interpret novel combinations of words. Child experimental studies have consistently shown that children are sensitive to such regularities from an early age, producing novel utterances that obey the mapping of arguments to syntactic positions in their language (Bowerman, 1982; Pinker, 1989; MacWhinney, 1995). However, it is not clear how they learn the item-specific and the more general associations between syntactic constructions and semantic interpretations. One aspect of language that provides a rich testbed for exploring such issues is the usage of verbs, specifically what syntactic constructions a verb can occur in. Verbs pose particular challenges to children in this regard, due to the complexity of their possible usages and the interacting semantic and syntactic factors that determine both the general patterns and the exceptions. In Section 5.1, we will discuss the acquisition of verb argument structure, including the theoretical and computational studies of this process in children.

In addition to the argument structure regularities, experiments with children have revealed strong associations between general semantic roles such as Agent and Destination, and syntactic positions such as subject and the prepositional object (e.g., Fisher, 1996, and related work). Despite the extensive use of semantic roles in various linguistic theories, there is little consensus on the nature of these roles. Moreover, it is not agreed upon how children learn general roles and their association with grammatical functions. Section 5.2 reviews linguistic theories and experimental findings on semantic roles, and computational models which simulate the process of learning the general conception of roles and their mapping to syntactic constituents in a sentence.

Finally, Section 5.3 focuses on the selectional restrictions or preferences imposed by a predicate term (mainly a verb) on its arguments, and common methodologies for representing and learning these preferences from corpus data.

5.1   ACQUISITION OF VERB ARGUMENT STRUCTURE

Verb argument structure is a complex aspect of language for a child to master, as it requires learning the relations of a verb to its arguments, or the participants in the event the verb describes. The argument structure of a verb determines the semantic relations of a verb to its arguments and how those arguments are mapped into valid syntactic expressions of the language. This complex aspect of language exhibits both general patterns across semantically similar verbs, as well as more idiosyncratic mappings of verbal arguments to syntactic forms. For example, many verbs which describe a change of state allow both an intransitive and a transitive form (e.g., *he broke the vase* or *the vase broke*). But for the verb *fall*, the transitive form is not allowed (*the vase fell*, but not *he fell the vase**).

The challenge of verb argument structure acquisition for children is to learn both the patterns that apply to large groups of verbs in each language, and the finer-grained semantic restrictions that govern the exceptions to these patterns. Given the number of verbs in the language and the wide range of syntactic structures that can be used to express verbal arguments, the acquisition of such knowledge is quite complex, and numerous questions remain concerning how children attain an adult level of competence.

As in other domains of language, behavioural patterns observed in young language learners can reveal clues about the underlying mechanisms involving the acquisition of argument structure. One such finding is a U-shaped learning curve similar to the one observed in children learning morphology (which we discussed in Section 4.1). After an early period of conservative behaviour where every verb is only produced in the context that it has been heard in before, children start to generalize the common argument structure patterns to novel cases. They may even overgeneralize the observed patterns, thereby producing incorrect forms such as *Don't you fall me down* (Bowerman, 1982). Eventually, such erroneous verb usages discontinue.

Various proposals have been put forward to account for the acquisition of verb argument structure, and the related empirical findings in children. With regard to language use, of particular interest has been how general and specific knowledge of verb argument structure interact to yield a U-shaped learning curve. The mechanisms that children use to recover from making overgeneralization errors have especially been the subject of much debate (Pinker, 1984, 1989; Bowerman, 1988, 1996; MacWhinney, 2004). This problem is of particular interest since the availability of negative evidence cannot be relied on in this process (Brown and Hanlon, 1970; Marcus, 1993).

As in other aspects of language acquisition, the association between syntactic forms and semantic content has been attributed to innate representations of linguistic knowledge. In the next section, we will review the *semantic bootstrapping* theory, a nativist account of learning form-meaning associations. In contrast, a number of usage-based theories on the acquisition of verb argument structure have been developed around the central theme of *construction grammar*. We will look at these theories in Section 5.1.2.

5.1.1   SEMANTIC BOOTSTRAPPING

The semantic bootstrapping hypothesis, proposed by Pinker (1984, 1989), is a nativist account specialized for verb argument structure acquisition. According to this hypothesis, the semantic roles of a verb are positions in decompositional representations of verbs' meanings (e.g., Agent is the first argument of CAUSE, Patient is the second argument of CAUSE, and Theme is the first argument of GO and BE), and each semantic role is associated with its own linking rule (e.g., Theme is linked to Subject if that syntactic function has not already been assigned, otherwise to Object). Moreover, the acquisition of lexical syntactic categories such as Noun and Verb is boosted by the semantic properties of their members; for example, by observing a scene, the child infers that the word referring to the event is a verb, and the word referring to an object present in the scene is a noun.

Since this model specifies that the way a verb's arguments are linked follows directly from its semantic representation, differences in the way closely related verbs (or alternative constructions involving the same verb) map their arguments must reflect differences in their meaning. Thus the perfect correspondence between a verb's semantic structure and the mapping of its arguments allows a child with innate linking rules to predict correct mappings once he knows what a verb means. This hypothesis has a number of theoretical flaws. The extraction of syntactic categories from the semantic representation is underspecified. There is no correspondence between these categories and observable semantic properties that is universal among natural languages. Furthermore, since the linking rules proposed by this model are general and apply equally to all verbs, they do not provide precise guidelines for the acquisition of phrase-structure rules and for predicting the subcategorization frames of newly acquired verbs. This means that the burden is on the child to learn these highly articulated semantic structures. Moreover, some recent psycholinguistic experiments question the effectiveness of such rules in acquiring verb argument structure and avoiding overgeneralization errors (e.g., Bowerman, 1990; Demuth *et al.*, 2002).

5.1.2   CONSTRUCTION GRAMMAR

A group of theories called *Construction Grammar* propose a different approach to the representation and acquisition of argument structure, by positing abstract constructions that pair any form (words, multi-word expressions, syntactic structures, etc.) with meaning, independently of the lexical items that appear in them (e.g., Lakoff, 1987; Fillmore *et al.*, 1988; Langacker, 1999). In particular, Goldberg (1995, 2006) defines an argument structure construction as a mapping between underlying verb-argument relations and the syntax used to express them. This is in stark contrast to the highly modular accounts of language learning, which posit syntax and semantics as units with different representational frameworks and acquisition timelines. Construction Grammar is also different from Semantic Bootstrapping in that it claims that the mapping between form and meaning is learned from observation, as opposed to relying on innate linking rules between the two.

Here is an example of an argument structure construction, the *Ditransitive Construction*, taken from Goldberg (1995):

Semantics: **X** Causes **Y to** Receive **Z**
Syntax: **Subj V Obj Obj$_2$**

The construction specifies that a ditransitive form implies a transfer of a theme between an agent and a receiver, and that the agent is realized as the subject of the sentence, the receiver as the first object, and the theme as the second object. *Mary gave Lil the book* is an instance of this construction. However, the meaning of the construction can be generalized to lexical items that are not a typical member of that construction, as in *Pat faxed Bill the letter*.

Goldberg (1995) offers an account of how the meaning associated with argument structure constructions is acquired: argument structure patterns are initially acquired on a verb-by-verb basis, and constructions associated with common syntactic patterns are learned through a process of categorization and generalization over the input. The generalization of constructional meaning is based largely on the meanings of highly frequent light verbs, i.e., highly frequent verbs with very general meanings such as *go, do, make, give, put*. Goldberg shows that the meanings of some of the light verbs correspond closely to the meanings associated with argument structure constructions. For example, the intransitive syntactic pattern **Subj V Obl** paired with the meaning **X** Moves **Y** corresponds to the meaning of the light verb *go*.

Bencini and Goldberg (2000) compare the role of the main verb and the argument structure construction in sentence meaning by asking a number of participants to sort sentences according to their meaning. The results suggest that adults probably see both verbs and constructions as relevant to determining meaning. An established form-meaning mapping may even impose an "unusual" meaning when a verb is used in a manner that is not typical for it. For example, in *the fly buzzed into the room*, using the verb *buzzed* in a construction with a path argument induces a semantics of movement as well as the standard sound emission sense for that verb.

5.1.3   COMPUTATIONAL MODELS OF CONSTRUCTION LEARNING

A few computational models have combined a nativist approach to learning form-meaning associations and a probabilistic method for adjusting the pre-structured representation of the linguistic knowledge with the input data. For example, Buttery (2003, 2004) presents Categorial Grammar Learner (CGL), a parameter-setting model that employs a Bayesian algorithm for acquiring a lexicon of words' syntactic and semantic properties. The argument structure of a predicate term is represented as a syntactic category constructed from a pre-defined set of primitive categories and two basic combining operators. At each point in learning, the hypothesis space is recorded as a hierarchy of (categorial and word order) parameters to be set. The model is tested on a subset of CHILDES for which a unification-based grammar description has been created. The model of Niyogi (2002) also uses a Bayesian algorithm for learning the syntactic and semantic properties of verbs. This model relies on extensive prior knowledge in the form of a Bayesian hypothesis space and the probabilities over it. The model shows effects of both syntactic and semantic bootstrapping—i.e., the use of syntax to aid in inducing the semantics of a verb, and the use of semantics to narrow down possible syntactic forms in which a verb can be expressed.

In contrast, several connectionist models have been proposed for learning associations between the semantic properties of verbs and their arguments and their syntactic behaviour from input data. Allen (1997), for example, presents a connectionist model for thematic role assignment which simulates the integration of syntactic, semantic and lexical information, including the number of arguments in the clause, the identity of the verb, the semantics of the verb, the presence and identity of any preposition, and the identity and order of arguments in the utterance. While simple local representations are used for verbs and prepositions in the utterance, a distributed representation of nouns is used to allow for generalization over semantic features. The network is trained on a collection of usages from the most frequent verbs in child-directed speech from CHILDES. Testing the network consists of supplying both grammatical and ungrammatical sentences as input. The model can distinguish between the grammatical and ungrammatical utterances, and it can predict the semantic properties of verbs and nouns. This model was later extended by Allen and Seidenberg (1999) to propose a theory of grammaticality judgment. The extended model is composed of a comprehension layer which can produce a semantic representation for a given sequence of input words, and a production layer which generates a sentence for a given input sequence of meaning symbols. The judgment process is modeled by querying the network for its version of an input sentence, and then comparing the match between the input and output forms. Similarly, the connectionist model of Desai (2002) learns the mapping between simple sentences in a miniature language and the representation of their relational meaning, with limited generalization capacity. However, the model demonstrates effects similar to syntactic and semantic bootstrapping, using a very restricted set of semantic features.

Other computational models have concentrated on the form-meaning mapping that must be acquired for verbs, specifically looking at the acquisition of constructions. Chang (2004, 2008) presents a model for learning lexically-specific multi-word constructions from annotated child-directed transcript data. The goal of the model is to learn associations between form relations and meaning relations, and to use them in language comprehension (we will review this model in more detail in the next section). In a simpler setting, Dominey (2003) and Dominey and Inui (2004) model the acquisition of grammatical constructions from utterances paired with video. Learning in this model is highly dependent on the assumption that each syntactic form uniquely identifies the associated meaning (i.e., forms and meanings are in a one-to-one mapping). Both models can generalize their acquired knowledge to new verbs, but their generalization abilities are limited, particularly when facing novel semantic combinations.

The Bayesian model of Alishahi and Stevenson (2008) proposes a novel representation for argument structure constructions as probabilistic associations between syntactic and semantic features of a verb usage. A Bayesian clustering algorithm is used to model the acquisition of constructions by detecting similar usages and grouping them together. Language use is modeled as a prediction problem: each language task is viewed as finding the best value for a missing feature in a usage, based on the available features in that same usage and the acquired knowledge of language so far. Computational simulations of the model show that its behaviour mirrors that of young children in some relevant aspects. The model demonstrates a conservative use of the more frequent usages for each individual verb at the beginning, followed by a phase when general patterns are grasped and applied overtly, which leads to occasional overgeneralization errors. Such errors cease to be made over time as the model processes more input. In a similar approach, Perfors *et al.* (2010) propose a hierarchical Bayesian model for the acquisition of argument structure constructions. This model also simulates the patterns of generalization observed in children. Moreover, the model makes inferences about the variability of verb constructions.

5.1.4   CASE STUDY: CHANG (2004)

Chang (2004) presents a model for learning lexically specific multi-word constructions from annotated child-directed transcript data. The goal of the model is to learn associations between form relations (typically word order) and meaning relations (typically role-filler bindings) from input data, and to use them in language comprehension. The learning task is defined as finding the best grammar to fit the observed data, given the space of possible grammars and a training corpus. The latter contains a sequence of examples of utterances paired with their context.

The space of possible grammars in this model is defined by a unification-based formalism called Embodied Construction Grammar (ECG). In this framework, both form and meaning are represented as subgraphs of elements and relations among them, and lexical constructions involve a simple mapping between these two subgraphs. The prior knowledge embedded in the model consists of conceptual knowledge (an ontology of typed feature structures or schemata for people, objects, locations and actions) and lexical knowledge (a set of lexical constructions represented in the ECG formalism, linking simple forms to specific conceptual items). The model uses a construction analyzer that identifies the constructions responsible for a given utterance based on partial parsing techniques. Learning (i.e., updating the grammar) includes forming new structured maps to account for mappings present in the input but unexplained by the current grammar, and merging similar constructions into a more general or a larger one. The minimum description length (MDL) heuristic is used to evaluate the proposed constructions in terms of the size of the final grammar and the cost of the data given the grammar.

A sample of a construction learned by the model can be seen in Fig. 5.1. The model learns only item-based constructions, and the only generalization learned over the input concerns the semantic constraints on the arguments (for example, THROW-BALL construction and THROW-BLOCK construction are merged into a general THROW-OBJECT construction). However, since this work is part of a larger project on language comprehension, it provides a testbed for applying the acquired knowledge in language understanding.

5.2   SEMANTIC ROLES AND GRAMMATICAL FUNCTIONS

Semantic roles such as Agent, Recipient and Instrument are a critical aspect of linguistic knowledge because they indicate the relations of the participants in an event to the main predicate. How children acquire this kind of complex relational knowledge, which links predicate-argument structure to

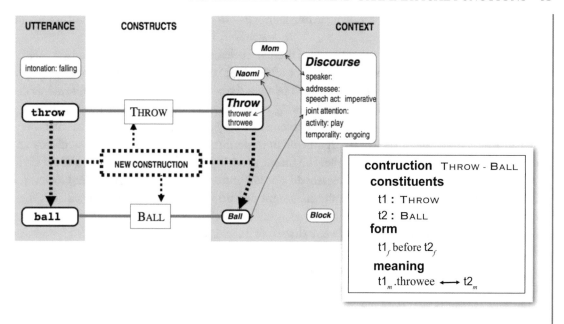

Figure 5.1: A sample construction learned by the model of Chang (2004).

syntactic expression, is still not well understood. Fundamental questions remain concerning how semantic roles are learned, and how associations are established between roles and the grammatical positions the role-bearing arguments appear in.

5.2.1   THE NATURE OF SEMANTIC ROLES

The notion of thematic roles was first introduced by semanticists as the relationship between a predicate and its arguments (Fillmore, 1968; Jackendoff, 1972). However, this notion was extensively used by syntacticians as a theoretical device to explain argument indexing (i.e., linking grammatical relations to semantic structure) and grammatical generalization (Chomsky, 1981; Pinker, 1984). In many theories of syntax such as Government and Binding Theory (Chomsky, 1981) and Lexical-Functional Grammar (Kaplan and Bresnan, 1982; Bresnan, 2001; Falk, 2001), thematic roles are believed to be discrete, limited in number, and universal.

   As we saw in Section 5.1.1, the mapping between roles and sentence structure are defined through a set of universal linking rules. These rules are argued to be innate and to help children in learning the syntax of their language. A strong version of these rules suggests that the mapping of a thematic role to a particular grammatical function is rigid (Pinker, 1984; Baker, 1988). A weaker position proposes that thematic roles and syntactic positions are matched by means of a hierarchy, such that the highest-ranked thematic role occupies the highest-ranked syntactic position (i.e., the subject), and one works one's way down the two hierarchies in parallel until one runs out of arguments (Grimshaw, 1990; VanValin and LaPolla, 1997; Jackendoff, 1990).

Many researchers have proposed lists of thematic roles, mostly different in size and granularity. But there is little consensus on the "correct" set of thematic roles. Even the familiar roles are subject to disagreement (for example, whether or not Theme is the same role as Patient). That is mainly due to the fact that, in order for the universal linking rules to be useful, it should be possible to assign each argument of every verb in the language to one and only one thematic role. That is, what a verb semantically entails about each of its arguments must permit us to assign the argument, clearly and definitely, to some role or other, and what the meaning entails about every argument must always be distinct enough that two arguments clearly do not fall under the same role definition. However, it seems that there is no cross-linguistically consistent definition of thematic roles that satisfies these criteria.

Dowty (1991) proposes a different theory of thematic roles: the Proto-Role Hypothesis. According to his theory, thematic roles draw from a pool of more basic semantic properties such as sentience, volition, and movement. No one thematic role necessarily has all of these properties, and some have more than others. The proposed proto-roles are based on analysis of linguistic data. However, Dowty (1991) does not give any explicit account on whether these proto-roles are innate or whether children actually learn them. Kako (2006) provides an experimental test of the Proto-Roles Hypothesis, and shows that human subjects assign the suggested proto-role properties to grammatical roles such as subject and object, even for a novel verb (or a familiar verb in an unusual construction).

Although several experimental studies have been performed to study thematic roles in language processing (see, for example, Trueswell et al. (1994)), there is little agreement on what the nature of thematic roles is. However, the experiments of McRae et al. (1997) on human subjects' ranking of role/filler featural similarity for Agent and Patient roles, as well as their ambiguity resolution in the presence of featural bias, suggests that thematic roles might best be viewed as verb-specific concepts. Based on such results, pioneers of usage-based language acquisition have suggested that children do not have access to a pre-defined set of thematic roles or proto-role properties. Instead, children learn thematic roles gradually and from the input they receive, through a process of categorization and generalization (e.g., Lieven et al., 1997; Tomasello, 2000). For instance, Tomasello (2000) claims that, initially, there are no general labels such as Agent and Theme, but rather verb-specific concepts such as 'hitter' and 'hittee,' or 'sitter' and 'thing sat upon.' It remains unexplained, though, precisely how verb-specific roles metamorphose to general semantic roles.

There are few experiments on how children learn general semantic roles. However, Shayan and Gershkoff-Stowe (2007) show that children indeed demonstrate a pattern of gradually learning thematic roles, and that both age and having access to linguistic cues affect the learning process. Moreover, experiments with children have revealed the use of verb-specific biases in argument interpretation (Nation et al., 2003), as well as of strong associations between general roles and syntactic positions (e.g., Fisher, 1996). However, the how and when of the emergence and learning of thematic roles is yet to be explored through further psycholinguistic experiments and computational modeling.

5.2.2   COMPUTATIONAL STUDIES OF SEMANTIC ROLES

In the computational linguistics literature, semantic role labeling of text corpora has been well studied. Many supervised models (e.g., Gildea and Jurafsky, 2002; Hacioglu *et al.*, 2004) have been proposed which use manually annotated corpora of PropBank (Palmer *et al.*, 2005) or FrameNet (Baker *et al.*, 1998) as training data. Unsupervised methods either use bootstrapping to learn frames for verbs (e.g., Riloff and Schmelzenbach, 1998), or a verb lexicon such as VerbNet (Kipper *et al.*, 2000) and a probability model to estimate the best role tag for each sentence constituent (Swier and Stevenson, 2004).

Many computational systems model human learning of the assignment of general pre-defined roles to sentence constituents, using a multi-feature representation of the semantic properties of arguments. McClelland and Kawamoto (1986) present one of the first models of this kind, a connectionist model for assigning roles to constituents of sentences using the surface structure of the sentence as the input. Words are represented as vectors of semantic features (*human, softness, gender,* etc., for nouns, and *cause, touch,* etc., for verbs). The output of the model is the assignment of a limited number of fixed thematic roles such as Agent and Instrument to the arguments of a verb. The model can also guess certain properties (semantic features) of a missing argument in a sentence, but the roles themselves are not learned. Morris *et al.* (2000) also present a connectionist model that assigns nouns (mostly proper names) to the appropriate roles for a number of sentence structures. Again, the model is trained on sentences annotated with the correct role assignment for their arguments, where a limited number of pre-defined roles (Agent, Indirect Patient, etc.) are used. Also (as we saw before in Section 5.1.3), Allen (1997) presents yet another connectionist model for thematic role assignment which simulates the integration of syntactic, semantic and lexical information. In this model, arguments are labeled with the appropriate role from a set of traditional thematic roles. Allen's model treats the representation of thematic roles differently in that each role is further elaborated by additional proto-role units. The network can predict the semantic features of novel verbs and the semantic roles (as well as the proto-role properties) for each argument in the input. However, the explicit labeling of the arguments is critical to the model, and it is not clear whether the model can learn these roles based only on the semantic properties of the arguments and the set of proto-role properties specified in the training data.

All of these models require explicit labeling of the arguments that receive the same role in order to learn the association of the roles to semantic properties and/or syntactic positions. However, a number of computational models learn verb-specific roles that are not generalized. For example as we saw in Section 5.1.4, the model of Chang (2004) learns associations between form and meaning relations from input data, but does not make any generalizations beyond the scope of one lexical entry and therefore does not learn a conception for a general semantic role. In contrast, Alishahi and Stevenson (2010) propose a probabilistic model of semantic role learning that can acquire associations between the semantic properties of the arguments of an event, and the syntactic positions that the arguments appear in. These probabilistic associations enable the model to learn general conceptions of roles based on exposure to individual verb usages, and without requiring explicit labeling of the roles in the input. We will review the details of this model in the next section.

Others have looked at learning the appropriate cues of the language for role assignment, such as word order, noun animacy, and case inflection. It is an interesting problem because such cues might or might not be present in every sentence, and one cue may conflict with another cue as to the correct role assignment. Models proposed by Bates and MacWhinney (1989) and Matessa and Anderson (2000) can both learn the cue dominance hierarchy of the language. The Competition Model of Bates and MacWhinney (1989) uses a learning-on-error mechanism, where a strength counter is maintained for each cue. In deciding a role, the noun with the largest total cue strength is assigned to that role. The Model of Matessa and Anderson (2000) uses both declarative and procedural rules for role assignment. This model predicts the roles assigned by human subjects better than the Competition model, but neither of the models learn an explicit profile for each role.

5.2.3   CASE STUDY: ALISHAHI AND STEVENSON (2010)

As seen in Section 5.1.3, Alishahi and Stevenson (2008) propose a Bayesian framework for learning and use of argument structure constructions in children. The model learns the argument structure frames for each verb, and their grouping across verbs into constructions. Alishahi and Stevenson (2010) expand this model to the acquisition of semantic roles. In contrast with the original version, the extended model does not assume that the child can perceive the "correct" semantic role for each argument upon watching an event. Instead, it assumes that the child can infer certain semantic properties for the arguments. As the model processes the input, it associates each argument of a predicate with a semantic profile, which is a probability distribution over a set of such semantic properties. Moreover, the model forms probabilistic associations between the semantic properties of the arguments, their syntactic positions, and the semantic primitives of the predicate. These associations are generalized (through the constructions) to form more abstract notions of role semantics, dependent on argument position and verb primitives. Fig. 5.2 shows a sample snapshot of the verb frames and constructions learned by this model.

Through computational simulation of their model, Alishahi and Stevenson (2010) show that initially the semantic profiles of an argument position yield verb-specific conceptualisations of the role associated with that position. As the model is exposed to more input, these verb-based roles gradually transform into more abstract representations that reflect the general properties of arguments across the observed verbs. They further establish that such representations can be useful in guiding the argument interpretation of ambiguous input, as well as in aiding word learning in unclear contexts.

5.3   SELECTIONAL PREFERENCES OF VERBS

Another important factor in the acceptability of a natural language sentence is the semantic restrictions or preferences imposed by the predicate terms in that sentence. Selectional preferences (or

constructions

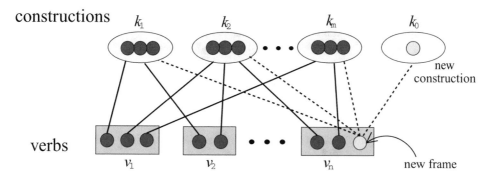

Figure 5.2: A sample snapshot of the verb frames and constructions learned by the model of Alishahi and Stevenson (2010).

constraints) are viewed as limitations on the applicability of natural language predicates to arguments. Many verbs show strong preferences concerning the semantic properties of their arguments. For example, *eating food* and *drinking water* are acceptable, whereas *eating water* and *drinking food* are normally not.

In their semantic theory, Katz and Fodor (1964) characterize selectional constraints as restrictions in terms of the defining features of the arguments: they outline a decompositional theory of word meaning in which lexical entries specify the features applicable to a particular lexical item. For words that denote predicates, Katz and Fodor propose that the arguments in their lexical entries be annotated with restrictions identifying the necessary and sufficient conditions that a semantically acceptable argument must meet. Such conditions are represented as Boolean functions of semantic features, such as HUMAN or HIGHER ANIMAL for the subject of the verb *hit*, and PHYSICAL OBJECT for its object. The lexical theory of Jackendoff (1983), on the other hand, situates selectional constraints as information appearing in the context of a rich representation of the predicate's meaning, such as the annotation LIQUID appearing as a constraint on one argument of the verb *drink*. Selectional constraints are sometimes explicitly integrated into the grammar, as in the Generative Lexicon Theory (Pustejovsky, 1995; Copestake and Briscoe, 1991). However, identifying restrictions that are both necessary and sufficient, and choosing the primitives themselves, is viewed by many to be an insurmountable problem.

Resnik (1993) instead emphasizes the view of the restrictions a verb places on its arguments as selectional preferences and proposes a different approach to their representation and learning. As we will see in the next section, this view has been adopted by many in the computational linguistics community. In this approach, the knowledge of words (or concepts) is represented as a pre-defined semantic class hierarchy, and statistical tools are used to learn selectional preferences from examples in a corpus. As opposed to a Boolean interpretation of selectional constraints, here the selectional preferences are viewed as probability distributions over various semantic classes. For example, the preferred objects of *eat* are represented not as the black-and-white class FOOD but rather as a gray probability distribution over all nouns or various classes thereof.

Many theories of lexical acquisition make use of selectional constraints (Gleitman and Gillette, 1995; Pinker, 1994). Gleitman and Gillette (1995) show that selectional constraints provide adult subjects with significant constraints on the possible meanings of unknown verbs: the subjects identified a verb 80% of the time if they were given the syntactic frame of the verb together with the nouns that appear as verb arguments; however, the syntactic frame alone or the noun arguments alone (without specifying their position) did not help subjects to identify the verb half the time. This shows that the semantic properties of the verb arguments (or verb selectional preferences) are more informative than simply the semantic associations between a verb and a group of nouns, or the syntactic properties of the verb. Moreover, selectional constraints play an important role in many aspects of language processing: they influence the syntactic structure of a sentence, especially in the face of ambiguity; they affect selecting the likely word in a sequence of speech signals, and they can be drawn on for the task of word sense disambiguation.

5.3.1   COMPUTATIONAL MODELS OF THE INDUCTION OF SELECTIONAL PREFERENCES

Two central questions for the automated treatment of selectional preferences are: what *representation* to use, and how to *induce* preferences from available data. A variety of computational models of verb selectional preferences have been proposed which use different statistical models to induce the preferences of each verb from corpus data. Most of these models, however, use the same representation for verb selectional preferences: the preference can be thought of as a mapping, with respect to an argument position for a verb, of each class to a real number (Light and Greiff, 2002). The induction of a verb's preferences is therefore modeled as using a set of training data to estimate that number.

Resnik (1993) is the first to model the problem of induction of selectional preferences using a pre-existing semantic class hierarchy, WordNet (Miller, 1990). He defines the selectional preference strength of a verb as the divergence between two probability distributions: the prior probabilities of the classes, and the posterior probabilities of the classes given that verb. The selectional association of a verb with a class is also defined as the contribution of that class to the total selectional preference strength. Resnik estimates the prior and posterior probabilities based on the frequencies of each verb and its relevant arguments in a corpus.

Following Resnik (1993, 1996), a number of methods were presented that make use of Word-Net and a text corpus, together with a variety of statistical models, to induce selectional preferences. Li and Abe (1998) model selectional preferences of a verb (for an argument position) as a probability distribution over set of nodes in WordNet. They use the Minimum Description Length (MDL) principle to find the best set for each verb and argument based on the usages of that verb in the training data. Clark and Weir (2002) also find an appropriate set of concept nodes to represent the selectional preferences for a verb, but do so using a χ^2 test over corpus frequencies mapped to concepts to determine when to generalize from a node to its parent. Ciaramita and Johnson (2000) use a Bayesian network with the same topology as WordNet to estimate the probability distribution of the relevant set of nodes in the hierarchy. Abney and Light (1999) use a different representational approach: they train a separate hidden Markov model for each verb, and the selectional preference is represented as a probability distribution over words instead of semantic classes.

In contrast to the WordNet-based methods above, Erk (2007) proposes a similarity-based model that does not rely on a hierarchical representation of semantic classes. Instead, her model estimates the selectional preference of a predicate argument position for a possible head word as a weighted sum of the similarities between that word and the head words for that argument position seen in a corpus. The similarity between the seen and the potential head word is computed based on a corpus-based semantic similarity metric.

It is not easy to evaluate the acquired selectional preferences on their own, since there is no "gold standard" set of examples against which to compare the outcome of a method (Light and Greiff, 2002). Existing models of verb selectional preference have been evaluated through a wide range of computational linguistic tasks, including word sense disambiguation (Resnik, 1997; Abney and Light, 1999; Ciaramita and Johnson, 2000; McCarthy and Carroll, 2003), PP-attachment disambiguation (Li and Abe, 1998); a pseudo-disambiguation task of choosing the best verb-argument pair (Clark and Weir, 2002), and semantic role labeling (Erk, 2007). Resnik (1996) also evaluated his method through two other tasks that are more interesting from a human language acquisition point of view: the simulation of plausibility judgements elicited from adult subjects, and the analysis of the way that arguments are syntactically realized for a class of English verbs.

5.4   SUMMARY

The acquisition of form-meaning associations in language has been studied less extensively compared to the acquisition of syntax. This is mainly due to a lack of proper resources for naturalistic semantic representations used by humans (and particularly children). However, several computational models have used artificially generated semantic features associated with natural language utterances. These models suggest that meaningful associations between syntactic forms and semantic features can be learned using proper statistical learning techniques. More importantly, probabilistic frameworks for representing and using these associations reflect a natural interaction between item-specific mappings of predicate terms and arguments on the one hand, and more general associations on the other hand. However, a detailed model of the acquisition of form-meaning associations that reflects the semantic complexities of naturalistic input data is still lacking.

CHAPTER 6

Final Thoughts

The questions that have been the focus of modern research on language are what knowledge of a language is, how this knowledge is acquired, and how it is used in comprehension and production (Chomsky, 1986; Seidenberg and MacDonald, 1999). Over the past few decades, computational tools and techniques have become increasingly popular as a useful tool for studying these questions. Computational cognitive modeling is a new and rapidly developing field, but during its short life span, it has been extensively beneficial to cognitive science in general, and the study of natural language acquisition and use in particular.

One of the main impacts of computational models of language acquisition has been to emphasize the importance of probabilistic knowledge and information theoretic methods in learning and processing language. The role of statistical methods in language acquisition was mainly ignored during the dominance of linguistic nativism, most famously by Chomsky (1975) who claimed that information theoretic methods cannot identify the set of grammatical sentences in linguistic data, and therefore are irrelevant to characterizing syntactic structure. However, the undeniable success of statistical techniques in processing linguistic data for more applied NLP tasks has provided strong evidence for their impact in human language acquisition (Chater and Manning, 2006). On the other hand, shallow probabilistic techniques which are not linguistically motivated can only go so far. For example, pure distributional models have been generally unsuccessful in accounting for learning a natural language in realistic scenarios. Fifty years after the development of the first computational models of language, hybrid modeling approaches that integrate deep structures with probabilistic inference seem to be the most promising direction for future research.

Developing computational algorithms that capture the complex structure of natural languages is still an open problem. There are several remaining challenges facing researchers regarding the research methods employed for computational studying of language, as well as the "framing" of the problems to be studied. We will take a look at some of these challenges in this chapter.

6.1 STANDARD RESEARCH METHODS

Computational studies of language combine research in linguistics, psychology and computer science. Because it is a young field of a highly interdisciplinary nature, the research methods employed by scholars are inevitably varied and non-standard. This is an unfortunate situation: it is often difficult to compare different models and analyze and compare their findings due to incompatible resources and evaluation techniques they employ. It is vital for the community to share resources and data collections, to develop unified schemes for annotation and information exchange, and to converge on standards for model comparison and evaluation.

As we discussed in Section 2.3.1, several large-scale corpora are now available and extensively used for supplying input data to implemented computational models of language (most notably CHILDES MacWhinney (1995)). The majority of these collections are text-based, and there are few resources available that provide semantic data. Isolated attempts have been made for collecting video recordings of experiments on children, or of naturalistic child–adult interactions (e.g., Roy, 2009). But these recordings are either unannotated, or they are marked with non-overlapping and non-standardized semantic features (e.g., gesture, gaze, objects in the scene) and therefore cannot be easily used by different computational modelers. The TalkBank project (MacWhinney *et al.*, 2004) is one such attempt at unifying the available multi-modal collections under a standardized data-sharing format.

When it comes to comparing and evaluating computational models, there is even less agreement among researchers in this field. The majority of algorithms used for simulating language acquisition are unsupervised, mainly because it is highly unrealistic to assume that children receive input data which is marked with the kind of linguistic knowledge they are supposed to learn. As a consequence, there is no gold standard for evaluating the outcome of these unsupervised models. Furthermore, the underlying representation of the linguistic knowledge in human brain is unknown; therefore, the knowledge of language that a model acquires cannot be evaluated on its own. Many models apply their acquired knowledge on different tasks, but such tasks are often chosen arbitrarily. With computational modeling becoming more widespread, it is extremely important for the community to converge on standard evaluation tasks and techniques in each domain.

6.2 LEARNING PROBLEMS

Due to the complex structure of natural languages, existing computational models have been focusing on restricted and isolated aspects of learning a language. Simplification is usually unavoidable when studying a complex problem, but the interaction between various aspects of linguistic knowledge and the timeline of their acquisition is one of the main open questions that needs to be investigated.

For example, learning the meaning of words is one of the basic steps of learning a language, and establishing the mapping between words and their correct meaning is a non-trivial task. In Chapter 3, we reviewed the main challenges facing child word learners and reviewed the computational approaches to studying this problem. However, it has been argued that the meaning of many words, especially verbs, cannot be learned without relying on syntactic cues. At the same time, learning the knowledge of syntax itself relies on knowing the meaning of (at least some) words. A promising research direction is to examine the mutual influence of word and syntax learning: the basic constructions of language can be acquired from a limited number of simple verbs whose meanings can be inferred through unambiguous contexts; the acquired constructions, in turn, can be used to guide learning the meaning of ambiguous words. Such a model can also be used to study the role of language on the development of conceptual structure, as is suggested by recent experimental findings (e.g., Choi and Bowerman, 1991). For example, speakers of different languages seem to have slightly different representations of spatial relations. Such effects can be studied in a unified model of word learning, where natural language sentences can be used as a cue for grouping relevant meaning elements that form a concept.

The study of language acquisition and language processing is another such example. Human language processing is a well-studied problem, and many computational models have been proposed for explaining the consistent patterns observed in human experimental data when processing language. But few models have attempted to integrate language acquisition and processing and study them in a unified framework. Instead, language acquisition and language processing have been mostly studied in isolation, a setting that is highly unrealistic. More comprehensive models of sentence processing must be developed that build on the acquired knowledge of linguistic constructions instead of pre-specified grammars.

Bibliography

Abney, S. and Light, M. (1999). Hiding a semantic hierarchy in a Markov model. In *Proceedings of the ACL Workshop on Unsupervised Learning in Natural Language Processing*. 67

Adriaans, P. (1992). *Language Learning from a Categorial Perspective*. Ph.D. thesis, Universiteit van Amsterdam. 51

Adriaans, P. (2001). Learning shallow context-free languages under simple distributions. In A. Copestake and K. Vermeulen, editors, *Algebras, Diagrams and Decisions in Language, Logic and Computation, CSLI/CUP*. CSLI, Stanford. 51

Akhtar, N. (1999). Acquiring basic word order: Evidence for data-driven learning of syntactic structure. *Journal of Child Language*, **26**, 339–356. DOI: 10.1017/S030500099900375X 4, 48

Alishahi, A. and Fazly, A. (2010). Integrating syntactic knowledge into a model of cross-situational word learning. In *Proceedings of the 32nd Annual Conference of the Cognitive Science Society*. 36

Alishahi, A. and Stevenson, S. (2008). A computational model of early argument structure acquisition. *Cognitive Science*, **32**(5), 789–834. DOI: 10.1080/03640210801929287 59, 64

Alishahi, A. and Stevenson, S. (2010). Learning general properties of semantic roles from uasge data: A computational model. *Language and Cognitive Processes*, **25**(1), 50–93. DOI: 10.1080/01690960902840279 63, 64, 65

Allen, J. (1997). Probabilistic constraints in acquisition. In A. Sorace, C. Heycock, and R. Shillcock, editors, *Proceedings of the GALA97 Conference on Language Acquisition, Edinburth*, pages 300–305. 49, 59, 63

Allen, J. and Seidenberg, M. S. (1999). The emergence of grammaticality in connectionist networks. In B. MacWhinney, editor, *Emergence of Language*. Lawrence Erlbaum Associates, Hillsdale, NJ. 49, 59

Angluin, D. (1988). *Identifying languages from stochastic examples*. Yale University, Dept. of Computer Science. 46

Baker, C. F., Fillmore, C. J., and Lowe, J. B. (1998). The Berkeley FrameNet project. In *Proceedings of the 36th Annual Meeting of the Association for Computational Linguistics and 17th International Conference on Computational Linguistics*. DOI: 10.3115/980845.980860 63

Baker, M. C. (1988). *Incorporation: A theory of grammatical function changing*. Chicago: University of Chicago Press. 61

Bannard, C., Lieven, E., and Tomasello, M. (2009). Modeling children's early grammatical knowledge. *Proceedings of the National Academy of Sciences*, **106**(41), 17284–17289. DOI: 10.1073/pnas.0905638106 51

Barrett, H. and Kurzban, R. (2006). Modularity in cognition: Framing the debate. *Psychological Review*, **113**(3), 628–647. DOI: 10.1037/0033-295X.113.3.628 2

Bates, E. and MacWhinney, B. (1989). Functionalism and the competition model. In B. MacWhinney and E. Bates, editors, *The crosslinguistic study of sentence processing*, pages 3–76. New York: Cambridge University Press. 64

Behrend, D. A. (1990). Constraints and development: A reply to Nelson (1998). *Cognitive Development*, **5**, 313–330. DOI: 10.1016/0885-2014(90)90020-T 3, 27

Bencini, G. M. L. and Goldberg, A. E. (2000). The contribution of argument structure constructions to sentence meaning. *Journal of Memory and Language*, **43**, 640–651. DOI: 10.1006/jmla.2000.2757 58

Berman, R. A., editor (2004). *Language development across childhood and adolescence*, volume 3 of *Trends in Language Acquisition Research*. John Benjamins, Amsterdam/Philadelphia. 1

Bloom, P. (2000). *How children learn the meanings of words*. The MIT Press. 27

Bod, R. (1992). A computational model of language performance: Data Oriented Parsing. In *Proceedings of the 14th International Conference on Computational Linguistics*, pages 855–859. Stroudsburg, PA: Association for Computational Linguistics. DOI: 10.3115/992383.992386 52

Bod, R. (2009). From exemplar to grammar: A probabilistic analogy-based model of language learning. *Cognitive Science*, **33**(4). DOI: 10.1111/j.1551-6709.2009.01031.x 52

Borensztajn, G., Zuidema, W., and Bod, R. (2009). Children's grammars grow more abstract with age–Evidence from an automatic procedure for identifying the productive units of language. *Topics in Cognitive Science*, **1**, 175–188. DOI: 10.1111/j.1756-8765.2008.01009.x 52

Bowerman, M. (1982). Evaluating competing linguistic models with language acquisition data: Implications of developmental errors with causative verbs. *Quaderni di semantica*, **3**, 5–66. 4, 8, 55, 56

Bowerman, M. (1988). The 'no negative evidence' problem. In J. Hawkins, editor, *Explaining language universals*. Londen: Blackwell. 56

Bowerman, M. (1990). Mapping thematic roles onto syntactic functions: Are children helped by innate linking rules? *Linguistics*, **28**, 1253–1289. DOI: 10.1515/ling.1990.28.6.1253 57

Bowerman, M. (1996). Argument structure and learnability: Is a solution in sight? In *Proceedings of the Berkeley Linguistics Society*, volume 22, pages 454–468. 56

Bresnan, J. (2001). *Lexical functional syntax*. Blackwell Textbooks in Linguistics. Blackwell Publishers. 61

Broen, P. A. (1972). *The verbal environment of the language-learning child*. American Speech and Hearing Association. 21

Brown, P., Mercer, R., Della Pietra, V., and Lai, J. (1992). Class-based n-gram models of natural language. *Computational Linguistics*, **18**(4), 467–479. 43

Brown, P. F., Della Pietra, S. A., Della Pietra, V. J., and Mercer, R. L. (1993). The mathematics of statistical machine translation: Parameter estimation. *Computational Linguistics*, **19**(2), 263–311. 29

Brown, R. (1973). *A first language: Ehe early stages*. Harvard University Press, Cambridge, Massachusetts. 1

Brown, R. and Hanlon, C. (1970). Derivational complexity and order of acquisition of syntax. *Cognition and the Development of Language, New York; Wiley*, pages 11–53. 45, 56

Burnard, L. (2000). Users reference guide for the British National Corpus. Technical report, Oxford University Computing Services. 21

Butterworth, G. (1991). The ontogeny and phylogeny of joint visual attention. In A. Whiten, editor, *Natural theories of mind: Evolution, development, and simulation of everyday mindreading*. Blackwell, Oxford, England. 37

Buttery, P. (2003). A computational model for first language acquisition. In *Proceedings of CLUK6, Edinburgh*, pages 1–8. 58

Buttery, P. (2004). A quantitative evaluation of naturalistic models of language acquisition: The efficiency of the Triggering Learning Algorithm compared to a Categorial Grammar Learner. In *Proceedings of the First Workshop on Psycho-computational Models of Human Language Acquisition*, pages 1–6. 58

Buttery, P. J. (2006). Computational models for first language acquisition. Technical Report UCAM-CL-TR-675, University of Cambridge, Computer Laboratory. 47

Carey, S. (1978). The child as word learner. In M. Halle, J. Bresnan, and G. A. Miller, editors, *Linguistic Theory and Psychological Reality*. The MIT Press. 25, 27

Carey, S. and Bartlett, E. (1978). Acquiring a single new word. *Papers and Reports on Child Language Development*, **15**, 17–29. 26

Carpenter, M., Nagell, K., Tomasello, M., Butterworth, G., and Moore, C. (1998). Social cognition, joint attention, and communicative competence from 9 to 15 months of age. *Monographs of the Society for Research in Child Development, 63(4)*. DOI: 10.2307/1166214 27

Cartwright, T. and Brent, M. (1997). Syntactic categorization in early language acquisition: Formalizing the role of distributional analysis. *Cognition*, **63**(2), 121–170. DOI: 10.1016/S0010-0277(96)00793-7 43

Chang, N. (2004). Putting meaning into grammar learning. In *Proceedings of the First Workshop on Psycho-computational Models of Human Language Acquisition*, pages 17–24. 59, 60, 61, 63

Chang, N. (2008). *Constructing grammar: A computational model of the emergence of early constructions.* Ph.D. thesis, University of California at Berkeley. 59

Chater, N. and Manning, C. D. (2006). Probabilistic models of language processing and acquisition. *Trends in Cognitive Science*, **10**(7), 335–344. DOI: 10.1016/j.tics.2006.05.006 19, 51, 69

Choi, S. and Bowerman, M. (1991). Learning to express motion events in English and Korean: The influence of language-specific lexicalization patterns. *Cognition*, **41**, 83–121. DOI: 10.1016/0010-0277(91)90033-Z 71

Chomsky, N. (1965). *Aspects of the theory of syntax.* The MIT Press. 2, 3, 45

Chomsky, N. (1975). *The logical structure of linguistic theory.* Plenum press. 69

Chomsky, N. (1980). *Rules and representations.* Oxford: Basil Blackwell. 2

Chomsky, N. (1981). *Lectures on government and binding.* Mouton de Gruyter. 4, 16, 45, 61

Chomsky, N. (1986). *Knowledge of language: Its nature, origin, and use.* Praeger Publishers. 3, 45, 69

Chouinard, M. M. and Clark, E. V. (2003). Adult reformulations of child errors as negative evidence. *Journal of Child Language*, **30**(3), 637–669. DOI: 10.1017/S0305000903005701 45

Christiansen, M. and Chater, N. (1999). Connectionist natural language processing: The state of the art. *Cognitive Science*, **23**(4), 417–437. DOI: 10.1207/s15516709cog2304_2 41

Chrupała, G. and Alishahi, A. (2010). How do children learn lexical categories? Online entropy-based modeling of category induction. In *Proceedings of the 14th Conference on Computational Natural Language Learning*, Uppsala, Sweden. 44

Chrupała, G., Dinu, G., and Van Genabith, J. (2008). Learning morphology with Morfette. In *Proceedings of the Sixth International Conference on Language Resources and Evaluation.* 40

Ciaramita, M. and Johnson, M. (2000). Explaining away ambiguity: Learning verb selectional preference with Bayesian networks. In *Proceedings of the 18th International Conference on Computational Linguistics.* DOI: 10.3115/990820.990848 66, 67

Clark, A. (2000). Inducing syntactic categories by context distribution clustering. In *Proceedings of the 2nd Workshop on Learning Language in Logic and the 4th Conference on Computational Natural Language Learning-Volume 7*, pages 91–94. Association for Computational Linguistics, Morristown, NJ, USA. DOI: 10.3115/1117601.1117621 43, 44

Clark, A. (2001). Unsupervised induction of stochastic context free grammars with distributional clustering. In *Proceedings of the conference on Computational Natural Language Learning, Toulouse, France*, pages 105–112. DOI: 10.3115/1117822.1117831 51

Clark, A. (2003). Combining distributional and morphological information for part of speech induction. In *Proceedings of 10th meeting of the European Chapter of the Association for Computational Linguistics*, pages 59–66. DOI: 10.3115/1067807.1067817 44

Clark, A. (2006). PAC-learning unambiguous NTS languages. In *Proceedings of the 8th International Colloquium on Grammatical Inference*, pages 59–71. Springer, Berlin. 51

Clark, A. and Lappin, S. (2010a). *Linguistic nativism and the poverty of stimulus*. Wiley Blackwell, Oxford and Malden, MA. 4, 46, 47

Clark, A. and Lappin, S. (2010b). Unsupervised learning and grammar induction. In A. Clark, C. Fox, and S. Lappin, editors, *The Handbook of Computational Linguistics and Natural Language Processing*. Wiley-Blackwell. 51

Clark, E. V. (2009). *First language acquisition*. Cambridge University Press, second edition. 12, 27, 45

Clark, R. (1992). The selection of syntactic knowledge. *Language Acquisition*, **2**(2), 83–149. DOI: 10.1207/s15327817la0202_1 47

Clark, S. and Weir, D. (2002). Class-based probability estimation using a semantic hierarchy. *Computational Linguistics*, **28**(2), 187–206. DOI: 10.1162/089120102760173643 66, 67

Collobert, R. and Weston, J. (2008). A unified architecture for natural language processing: Deep neural networks with multitask learning. In *Proceedings of the 25th international conference on Machine learning*, pages 160–167. ACM. 50

Coltheart, M. (1999). Modularity and cognition. *Trends in Cognitive Sciences*, **3**(3), 115–120. DOI: 10.1016/S1364-6613(99)01289-9 2

Copestake, A. and Briscoe, T. (1991). Lexical operations in a unification-based framework. *Lecture Notes in Computer Science*, **627**, 101–119. 65

Cullicover, P. W. (1999). *Syntactic nuts*. Oxford University Press. 18

Daugherty, K. and Seidenberg, M. (1992). Rules or connections? The past tense revisited. In *Annual Conference of the Cognitive Science Society*, volume 14, pages 259–264. 41

De La Higuera, C. (1997). Characteristic sets for polynomial grammatical inference. *Machine Learning*, **27**(2), 125–138. DOI: 10.1023/A:1007353007695 46

Demuth, K., Machobane, M., Moloi, F., and Odato, C. (2002). Rule learning and lexical frequency effects in learning verb-argument structure. In *Proceedings of the 26th Annual Boston University Conference on Language Development*, pages 142–153. 57

Desai, R. (2002). Bootstrapping in miniature language acquisition. In *Proceedings of the 4th International Conference on Cognitive Modelling*. DOI: 10.1016/S1389-0417(01)00040-7 49, 59

Dominey, P. and Boucher, J. (2005). Learning to talk about events from narrated video in a construction grammar framework. *Artificial Intelligence*, **167**(1-2), 31–61. DOI: 10.1016/j.artint.2005.06.007 21

Dominey, P. F. (2003). Learning grammatical constructions in a miniature language from narrated video events. In *Proceedings of the 25nd Annual Conference of the Cognitive Science Society*. 59

Dominey, P. F. and Inui, T. (2004). A developmental model of syntax acquisition in the construction grammar framework with cross-linguistic validation in English and Japanese. In *Proceedings of the First Workshop on Psycho-computational Models of Human Language Acquisition*, pages 33–40. 59

Dowty, D. (1991). Thematic proto-roles and argument selection. *Language*, **67**(3), 547–619. DOI: 10.2307/415037 62

Dresher, B. and Kaye, J. (1990). A computational learning model for metrical phonology. *Cognition*, **34**(2), 137. DOI: 10.1016/0010-0277(90)90042-I 47

Elman, J. L. (1990). Finding structure in time. *Cognitive Science*, **14**, 179–211. DOI: 10.1207/s15516709cog1402_1 17, 49, 50

Elman, J. L. (1991). Distributed representation, simple recurrent networks, and grammatical structure. *Machine Learning*, **7**, 195–225. DOI: 10.1023/A:1022699029236 17, 49, 50

Erk, K. (2007). A simple, similarity-based model for selectional preferences. In *Proceedings of the 45th Annual Meeting of the Association of Computational Linguistics*, pages 216–223, Prague, Czech Republic. 67

Falk, Y. N. (2001). *Lexical-Functional Grammar: An introduction to parallel constraint-based syntax*. CSLI Publications. 61

Fazly, A., Alishahi, A., and Stevenson, S. (2008). A probabilistic incremental model of word learning in the presence of referential uncertainty. In *Proceedings of the 30th Annual Conference of the Cognitive Science Society*. 36

Fazly, A., Alishahi, A., and Stevenson, S. (2010).   A probabilistic computational model of cross-situational word learning.   *Cognitive Science*, **34**(6), 1017–1063. DOI: 10.1111/j.1551-6709.2010.01104.x 29, 33, 35

Fernard, A. (1992). Human maternal vocalizations to infants as biologically relevant signals: An evolutionary perspective. In *The Adaptive Mind*. Oxford University Press. 37

Fillmore, C. (1968). The case for case. In E. Back and R. J. Harms, editors, *Universals in linguistic theory*, pages 1–88. Holt, Rinehart and Winston. 61

Fillmore, C., Kay, P., and O'Connor, M. K. (1988). Regularity and idiomaticity in grammatical constructions: The case of *let alone*. *Language*, **64**, 501–538. DOI: 10.2307/414531 57

Fisher, C. (1996). Structural limits on verb mapping: The role of analogy in children's interpretations of sentences. *Cognitive Psychology*, **31**(1), 41–81. DOI: 10.1006/cogp.1996.0012 9, 55, 62

Fleischman, M. and Roy, D. (2005). Intentional context in situated language learning. In *Ninth Conference on Computational Natural Language Learning*. DOI: 10.3115/1706543.1706562 29

Fodor, J. (1998).   Unambiguous triggers.   *Linguistic Inquiry*, **29**(1), 1–36. DOI: 10.1162/002438998553644 47

Fodor, J. A. (1983). *The Modularity of Mind: An Essay on Faculty Psychology*. The MIT Press. 2

Francis, W., Kučera, H., and Mackie, A. (1982). *Frequency analysis of English usage: Lexicon and grammar*. Houghton Mifflin Harcourt (HMH). 21

Frank, M., Goodman, N., and Tenenbaum, J. (2007). A Bayesian framework for cross-situational word learning. *Advances in Neural Information Processing Systems*, **20**. 20, 29, 37

Frank, S., Goldwater, S., and Keller, F. (2009). Evaluating models of syntactic category acquisition without using a gold standard. In *Proceedings of the 31st annual meeting of the Cognitive Science Society*. 44

Frazier, L. (1979). *On comprehending sentences: Syntactic parsing strategies*. Unpublished doctoral dissertation, University of Connecticut. 51

Frazier, L. and Fodor, J. D. (1978). The sausage machine: A new two-stage parsing model. *Cognition*, **13**, 187–222. DOI: 10.1016/0010-0277(83)90022-7 16, 51

Freudenthal, D., Pine, J., and Gobet, F. (2006). Modelling the development of children's use of optional infinitives in English and Dutch using MOSAIC. *Cognitive Science*, **30**, 277–310. DOI: 10.1207/s15516709cog0000_47 53

Freudenthal, D., Pine, J., and Gobet, F. (2007). Understanding the developmental dynamics of subject omission: The role of processing limitations in learning. *Journal of Child Language*, **34**(01), 83–110. DOI: 10.1017/S0305000906007719 53

Freudenthal, D., Pine, J., and Gobet, F. (2009). Simulating the referential properties of Dutch, German, and English root infinitives in MOSAIC. *Language Learning and Development*, **5**(1), 1–29. DOI: 10.1080/15475440802502437 53

Gelman, S. and Taylor, M. (1984). How two-year-old children interpret proper and common names for unfamiliar objects. *Child Development*, pages 1535–1540. DOI: 10.2307/1130023 36, 41

Gertner, Y., Fisher, C., and Eisengart, J. (2006). Learning words and rules: Abstract knowledge of word order in early sentence comprehension. *Psychological Science*, **17**(8), 684–691. DOI: 10.1111/j.1467-9280.2006.01767.x 36

Gibson, E. and Wexler, K. (1994). Triggers. *Linguistic Inquiry*, **25**, 407–454. 16, 47

Gildea, D. and Jurafsky, D. (2002). Automatic labeling of semantic roles. *Computational Linguistics*, **23**(3), 245–288. DOI: 10.1162/089120102760275983 63

Gleitman, L. (1990). The structural sources of verb meanings. *Language Acquisition*, **1**, 135–176. DOI: 10.1207/s15327817la0101_2 25, 26, 36

Gleitman, L. and Gillette, J. (1995). The role of syntax in verb learning. In *Handbook of Child Language*. Oxford: Blackwell. 66

Gobet, F., Freudenthal, D., and Pine, J. M. (2004). Modelling syntactic development in a cross-linguistic context. In *Proceedings of the First Workshop on Psycho-computational Models of Human Language Acquisition*, pages 53–60. 51, 52, 53

Godfrey, J., Holliman, E., and McDaniel, J. (1992). SWITCHBOARD: Telephone speech corpus for research and development. In *1992 IEEE International Conference on Acoustics, Speech, and Signal Processing, 1992. ICASSP-92.*, volume 1. DOI: 10.1109/ICASSP.1992.225858 21

Gold, E. M. (1967). Language identification in the limit. *Information and Control*, **10**(5), 447–474. DOI: 10.1016/S0019-9958(67)91165-5 4, 46

Goldberg, A. (2006). *Constructions at work*. Oxford University Press Oxford, United Kingdom:. 57

Goldberg, A. E. (1995). *Constructions: A construction grammar approach to argument structure*. The University of Chicago Press. 57, 58

Goldsmith, J. (2001). Unsupervised learning of the morphology of a natural language. *Computational Linguistics*, **27**(2), 153–198. DOI: 10.1162/089120101750300490 40

Golinkoff, R. M., Hirsh-Pasek, K., Bailey, L. M., and Wegner, N. R. (1992). Young children and adults use lexical principles to learn new nouns. *Developmental Psychology*, **28**(1), 99–108. DOI: 10.1037/0012-1649.28.1.99 27

Gomez, R. and Gerken, L. (1999). Artificial grammar learning by 1-year-olds leads to specific and abstract knowledge. *Cognition*, **70**(2), 109–135. DOI: 10.1016/S0010-0277(99)00003-7 36

Grimshaw, J. (1990). *Argument structure*. Cambridge, MA: The MIT Press. 62

Hacioglu, K., Pradhan, S., Ward, W., Martin, J., and Jurafsky, D. (2004). Semantic role labeling by tagging syntactic chunks. In *Proceedings of CoNLL 2004 Shared Task*. 63

Hahn, U. and Nakisa, R. (2000). German inflection: Single route or dual route? *Cognitive Psychology*, **41**(4), 313–360. DOI: 10.1006/cogp.2000.0737 40

Hoff, E. and Naigles, L. (2002). How children use input to acquire a lexicon. *Child Development*, **73**(2), 418–433. DOI: 10.1111/1467-8624.00415 27, 37

Horning, J. (1972). A procedure for grammatical inference. *Information Processing*, **71**, 519–523. 46

Horst, J. S. and Samuelson, L. K. (2008). Fast mapping but poor retention by 24-month-old infants. *Infancy*, **13**(2), 128–157. DOI: 10.1080/15250000701795598 28

Horst, J. S., McMurray, B., and Samuelson, L. K. (2006). Online processing is essential for learning: Understanding fast mapping and word learning in a dynamic connectionist architecture. In *Proceedings of the 28th annual meeting of the Cognitive Science Society*. 28

Huttenlocher, J., Haight, W., Bryk, A., Seltzer, M., and Lyons, T. (1991). Early vocabulary growth: Relation to language input and gender. *Developmental Psychology*, **27**(2), 236–248. DOI: 10.1037/0012-1649.27.2.236 26

Jackendoff, R. (1972). *Semantic interpretation in generative grammar*. The MIT Press. 61

Jackendoff, R. (1983). *Semantics and cognition*. Cambridge, MA: The MIT Press. 65

Jackendoff, R. (1990). *Semantic structures*. Cambridge, MA: The MIT Press. 62

Jain, S. (1999). *Systems that learn: An introduction to learning theory*. The MIT Press. 46

Jones, G., Gobet, F., and Pine, J. M. (2000). A process model of children's early verb use. In *Proceedings of the 22th Annual Conference of the Cognitive Science Society*. 51, 52, 53

Jurafsky, D. (1996). A probabilistic model of lexical and syntactic access and disambiguation. *Cognitive Science*, **20**, 137–194. DOI: 10.1207/s15516709cog2002_1 18

Jurafsky, D. and Martin, J. (2003). *Speech and language processing: An introduction to natural language processing, computational linguistics, and speech recognition*. The MIT Press. 18

Kako, E. (2006). Thematic role properties of subjects and objects. *Cognition*, **101**, 1–42. DOI: 10.1016/j.cognition.2005.08.002 62

Kamhi, A. G. (1986). The elusive first word: The importance of the naming insight for the development of referential speech. *Jounal of Child Language*, **13**, 155–161. DOI: 10.1017/S0305000900000362 26, 27

Kaplan, R. and Bresnan, J. (1982). Lexical functional grammar: A formal system for grammatical representation. In J. Bresnan, editor, *The Mental Representation of Grammatical Relations*, pages 173–281. The MIT Press, Cambridge, Mass. 61

Kayne, R. (2000). *Parameters and universals*. Oxford University Press, USA. 47

Kemp, N., Lieven, E., and Tomasello, M. (2005). Young children's knowledge of the "Determiner" and "Adjective" categories. *Journal of Speech, Language and Hearing Research*, **48**(3), 592–609. DOI: 10.1044/1092-4388(2005/041) 36, 41

Kipper, K., Dang, H. T., and Palmer, M. (2000). Class-based construction of a verb lexicon. In *Proceedings of the 17th AAAI Conference*, pages 691–696. 63

Klein, D. and Manning, C. (2002). A generative constituent-context model for improved grammar induction. In *Proceedings of the 40th Annual Meeting of the Association for Computational Linguistics, Philadelphia, US*, pages 128–135. DOI: 10.3115/1073083.1073106 51

Kutas, M. and Hillyard, S. (1983). Event-related brain potentials to grammatical errors and semantic anomalies. *Memory & Cognition*, **11**(5), 539–550. 24

Lakoff, G. (1987). *Women, fire and dangerous things: What categories reveal about the mind*. Chicago: University of Chicago Press. 57

Landau, B., Smith, L. B., and Jones, S. (1998). Object shape, object function, and object name. *Journal of Memory and Language*, **38**(1), 1–27. DOI: 10.1006/jmla.1997.2533 26

Langacker, R. (1999). *Grammar and conceptualization*. Berlin: Mouton de Gruyter. 57

Lappin, S. and Shieber, S. M. (2007). Machine learning theory and practice as a source of insight into universal grammar. *Journal of Linguistics*, **43**, 1–34. DOI: 10.1017/S0022226707004628 51

Leech, G. (1992). 100 million words of English: The British National Corpus (BNC). *Language Research*, **28**(1), 1–13. 21

Legate, J. and Yang, C. (2002). Empirical re-assessment of stimulus poverty arguments. *Linguistic Review*, **19**(1/2), 151–162. DOI: 10.1515/tlir.19.1-2.151 4

Leonard, L. (2000). *Children with specific language impairment*. The MIT Press. 2

Lewis, M. P., editor (2009). *Ethnologue: Languages of the world*. Dallas, Tex.: SIL International, sixteenth edition. 1

Li, H. and Abe, N. (1998). Generalizing case frames using a thesaurus and the MDL principle. *Computational Linguistics*, **24**(2), 217–244. 66, 67

Li, P., Farkas, I., and MacWhinney, B. (2004). Early lexical development in a self-organizing neural network. *Neural Networks*, **17**, 1345–1362. DOI: 10.1016/j.neunet.2004.07.004 28

Li, P., Xiaowei, and MacWhinney, B. (2007). Dynamic self-organization and early lexical development in children. *Cognitive Science*, **31**, 581–612. DOI: 10.1080/15326900701399905 28, 29

Lieven, E., Behrens, H., Speares, J., and Tomasello, M. (2003). Early syntactic creativity: A usage-based approach. *Journal of Child Language*, **30**(02), 333–370. DOI: 10.1017/S0305000903005592 48

Lieven, E. V. M., Pine, J. M., and Baldwin, G. (1997). Lexically-based learning and early grammatical development. *Journal of Child Language*, **24**, 187–219. DOI: 10.1017/S0305000996002930 62

Light, M. and Greiff, W. (2002). Statistical models for the induction and use of selectional preferences. *Cognitive Science*, **26**(3), 269–281. DOI: 10.1207/s15516709cog2603_4 66, 67

Littschwager, J. C. and Markman, E. M. (1994). Sixteen- and 24-month-olds' use of mutual exclusivity as a default assumption in second-label learning. *Developmental Psychology*, **30**(6), 955–968. DOI: 10.1037/0012-1649.30.6.955 26

MacWhinney, B. (1982). Basic syntactic processes. In S. Kuczaj, editor, *Language Development: Syntax and Semantics*, volume 1, pages 73–136. Hillsdale, N.J., Lawrence Erlbaum. 4

MacWhinney, B. (1987). The competition model. In B. MacWhinney, editor, *Mechanisms of language acquisition*. Hillsdale, NJ: Erllbaum. 4, 48

MacWhinney, B. (1989). Competition and lexical categorization. In R. Corrigan, F. Eckman, and M. Noonan, editors, *Linguistic Categorization*, Current Issues in Linguistic Theory, pages 195–242. New York. John Benjamins. 28

MacWhinney, B. (1995). *The CHILDES project: tools for analyzing talk*. Hillsdale, NJ: Lawrence Erlbaum Associates, second edition. 8, 20, 21, 22, 55, 70

MacWhinney, B. (2004). A multiple process solution to the logical problem of language acquisition. *Journal of Child Language*, **31**, 883–914. DOI: 10.1017/S0305000904006336 4, 56

MacWhinney, B., Bird, S., Cieri, C., and Martell, C. (2004). TalkBank: Building an open unified multimodal database of communicative interaction. In *Proceedings of the Fourth International Conference on Language Resources and Evaluation, Lisbon*, pages 525–528. 20, 70

Manning, C. and Schütze, H. (1999). *Foundations of statistical natural language processing*. The MIT Press. 18

Marcus, G. F. (1993). Negative evidence in language acquisition. *Cognition*, **46**, 53–85. DOI: 10.1016/0010-0277(93)90022-N 4, 45, 56

Marcus, G. F., Pinker, S., Ullman, M., Hollander, M., Rosen, T. J., and Xu, F. (1992). Overregularization in language acquisition. *Monographs of the Society for Research in Child Development*, **57**(4, Serial No. 228). DOI: 10.2307/1166115 4, 21, 41

Marcus, M., Santorini, B., and Marcinkiewicz, M. (1994). Building a large annotated corpus of English: The Penn Treebank. *Computational Linguistics*, **19**(2), 313–330. 21

Markman, E. M. (1989). *Categorization and naming in children*. The MIT Press. 34

Markman, E. M. and Wachtel, G. F. (1988). Children's use of mutual exclusivity to constrain the meanings of words. *Cognitive Psychology*, **20**, 121–157. DOI: 10.1016/0010-0285(88)90017-5 3, 27

Marr, D. (1982). *Vision*. San Francisco, CA: W. H. Freeman. 12

Matessa, M. and Anderson, J. R. (2000). Modelling focused learning in role assignment. *Language and Cognitive Processes*, **15**(3), 263–292. DOI: 10.1080/016909600386057 64

Maurits, L., Perfors, A. F., and Navarro, D. J. (2009). Joint acquisition of word order and word reference. In *Proceedings of the 31st Annual Conference of the Cognitive Science Society*. 36

Mazzocco, M. M. M. (1997). Children's interpretations of homonyms: A developmental study. *Journal of Child Language*, **24**, 441–467. DOI: 10.1017/S0305000997003103 26

McCarthy, D. and Carroll, J. (2003). Disambiguating nouns, verbs, and adjectives using automatically acquired selectional preferences. *Computational Linguistics*, **29**(4), 639–654. DOI: 10.1162/089120103322753365 67

McClelland, J. L. and Kawamoto, A. H. (1986a). *Mechanisms of sentence processing: Assigning roles to constituents of sentences*, pages 272–325. The MIT Press Cambridge, MA, USA. 49, 63

McLeod, P., Plunkett, K., and Rolls, E. (1998). *Introduction to connectionist modelling of cognitive processes*. Oxford University Press, Oxford. 17

McNeill, D. (1966). The creation of language by children. *Psycholinguistic papers*, pages 99–115. 45

McRae, K., Ferretti, T. R., and Amyote, L. (1997). Thematic roles as verb-specific concepts. *Language and Cognitive Processes*, **12**(2/3), 137–176. DOI: 10.1080/016909697386835 62

Merriman, W. E. (1999). Competition, attention, and young children's lexical parsing. In B. MacWhinney, editor, *The emergence of language*, pages 331–358. Lawrence Erlbaum Associates, Mahwah, NJ. 28

Miller, G. (1990). WordNet: An on-line lexical database. *International Journal of Lexicography*, **17**(3). 66

Mintz, T. (2002). Category induction from distributional cues in an artificial language. *Memory and Cognition*, **30**(5), 678–686. 42

Mintz, T. (2003). Frequent frames as a cue for grammatical categories in child directed speech. *Cognition*, **90**(1), 91–117. DOI: 10.1016/S0010-0277(03)00140-9 21, 42, 44

Monaghan, P. and Mattock, K. (2009). Cross-situational language learning: The effects of grammatical categories as constraints on referential labeling. In *Proceedings of the 31st Annual Conference of the Cognitive Science Society*. 27

Morris, W. C., Cottrell, G. W., and Elman, J. L. (2000). A connectionist simulation of the empirical acquisition of grammatical relations. In S. Wermter and R. Sun, editors, *Hybrid neural symbolic integration*. Springer Verlag. 63

Naigles, L. and Hoff-Ginsberg, E. (1995). Input to verb learning: Evidence for the plausibility of syntactic bootstrapping. *Developmental Psychology*, **31**(5), 827–37. DOI: 10.1037/0012-1649.31.5.827 36

Nakisia, R., Plunkett, K., and Hahn, U. (2000). Single-and dual-route models of inflectional morphology. *Models of language acquisition: Inductive and deductive approaches*, pages 201–222. 40

Nation, K., Marshall, C. M., and Altmann, G. T. M. (2003). Investigating individual differences in children's real-time sentence comprehension using language-mediated eye movements. *Journal of Experimental Child Psych.*, **86**, 314–329. DOI: 10.1016/j.jecp.2003.09.001 62

Neuvel, S. and Fulop, S. (2002). Unsupervised learning of morphology without morphemes. In *Proceedings of the ACL workshop on Morphological and phonological learning-Volume 6*, pages 31–40. Association for Computational Linguistics. DOI: 10.3115/1118647.1118651 40

Ninio, A. (1980). Picture-book reading in mother–infant dyads belonging to two subgroups in Israel. *Child Development*, **51**, 587–590. DOI: 10.2307/1129299 27

Niyogi, S. (2002). Bayesian learning at the syntax-semantics interface. In *Proceedings of the 24th Annual Conference of the Cognitive Science Society*. 36, 58

Olguin, R. and Tomasello, M. (1993). Twenty-five-month-old children do not have a grammatical category of verb. *Cognitive Development*, **8**(3), 245–272. DOI: 10.1016/S0885-2014(93)80001-A 48

Onnis, L., Roberts, M., and Chater, N. (2002). Simplicity: A cure for overgeneralizations in language acquisition? In *Proceedings of the 24th Annual Conference of the Cognitive Science Society*, pages 720–725. 52

Palmer, M., Gildea, D., and Kingsbury, P. (2005). The proposition bank: An annotated corpus of semantic roles. *Computational Linguistics*, **31**(1), 71–106. DOI: 10.1162/0891201053630264 63

Pan, B. A., Rowe, M. L., Singer, J. D., and Snow, C. E. (2005). Maternal correlates of growth in toddler vocabulary production in low-income families. *Child Development*, **76**(4), 763–782. DOI: 10.1111/1467-8624.00498-i1 27, 37

Parisien, C., Fazly, A., and Stevenson, S. (2008). An incremental Bayesian model for learning syntactic categories. In *Proceedings of the Twelfth Conference on Computational Natural Language Learning*. DOI: 10.3115/1596324.1596340 43, 44

Pereira, F. (2000). Formal grammar and information theory: Together again? In *Philosophical Transactions of the Royal Society*, pages 1239–1253. Royal Society, London. 51

Perfors, A., Tenenbaum, J., and Regier, T. (2006). Poverty of the stimulus? A rational approach. In *Proceedings of the 28th annual conference of the cognitive science society*, pages 663–668. 51

Perfors, A., Tenenbaum, J., and Wonnacott, E. (2010). Variability, negative evidence, and the acquisition of verb argument constructions. *Journal of Child Language*, **37**, 607–642. DOI: 10.1017/S0305000910000012 60

Pinker, S. (1984). *Language learnability and language development*. Cambridge, MA: Harvard University Press. 56, 57, 61

Pinker, S. (1989). *Learnability and cognition: The acquisition of argument structure*. Cambridge, MA: MIT Press. 8, 27, 55, 56, 57

Pinker, S. (1991). Rules of language. *Science*, **253**(5019), 530. DOI: 10.1126/science.1857983 41, 42

Pinker, S. (1994). How could a child use verb syntax to learn verb semantics? *Lingua*, **92**, 377–410. DOI: 10.1016/0024-3841(94)90347-6 3, 66

Pinker, S. (1997). *How the mind works*. NY:Norton. 2

Plunkett, K. and Marchman, V. (1991). U-shaped learning and frequency effects in a multi-layered perception: Implications for child language acquisition. *Cognition*, **38**(1), 43–102. DOI: 10.1016/0010-0277(91)90022-V 40, 41

Plunkett, K., Sinha, C., Moller, M., and Strandsby, O. (1992). Symbol grounding or the emergence of symbols? Vocabulary growth in children and a connectionist net. *Connection Science*, **4**, 293–312. DOI: 10.1080/09540099208946620 28

Prasada, S. and Pinker, S. (1993). Generalisation of regular and irregular morphological patterns. *Language and Cognitive Processes*, **8**(1), 1–56. DOI: 10.1080/01690969308406948 40, 41

Pullum, G. and Scholz, B. (2002). Empirical assessment of stimulus poverty arguments. *Linguistic Review*, **19**(1/2), 9–50. DOI: 10.1515/tlir.19.1-2.9 4

Pustejovsky, J. (1995). *The generative lexicon*. Cambridge, MA: The MIT Press. 65

Quine, W. (1960). *Word and object*. Cambridge, MA: The MIT Press. 25, 27

Redington, M., Crater, N., and Finch, S. (1998). Distributional information: A powerful cue for acquiring syntactic categories. *Cognitive Science*, **22**(4), 425–469. DOI: 10.1207/s15516709cog2204_2 43, 44

Regier, T. (2005). The emergence of words: Attentional learning in form and meaning. *Cognitive Science*, **29**, 819–865. DOI: 10.1207/s15516709cog0000_31 26, 28, 29, 30, 31, 34

Resnik, P. (1993). *Selection and information: A class-based approach to lexical relationships*. Ph.D. thesis, University of Pennsylvania. 65, 66

Resnik, P. (1996). Selectional constraints: An information-theoretic model and its computational realization. *Cognition*, **61**, 127–199. DOI: 10.1016/S0010-0277(96)00722-6 66, 67

Resnik, P. (1997). Selectional preference and sense disambiguation. In *Proceedings of ACL Siglex Workshop on Tagging Text with Lexical Semantics, Why, What and How?, Washington, April 4-5, 1997*. DOI: 10.1017/S0305000910000012 67

Reznick, J. S. and Goldfield, B. A. (1992). Rapid change in lexical development in comprehension and production. *Developmental Psychology*, **28**(3), 406–413. DOI: 10.1037/0012-1649.28.3.406 26

Riloff, E. and Schmelzenbach, M. (1998). An empirical approach to conceptual case frame acquisition. In *Proceedings of the 6th Workshop on Very Large Corpora*, pages 49–56. 63

Rissanen, J. (1978). Modeling by shortest data description. *Automatica*, **14**(5), 465–471. DOI: 10.1016/0005-1098(78)90005-5 18

Roark, B. and Sproat, R. (2007). *Computational approaches to syntax and morphology*. Oxford University Press, Oxford. 40

Rosch, E., Mervis, C. B., Gray, W. D., Johnson, D. M., and Boyes-Braem, P. (1976). Basic objects in natural categories. *Cognitive Psychology*, **8**, 382–439. DOI: 10.1016/0010-0285(76)90013-X 34

Roy, D. (2009). New horizons in the study of child language acquisition. In *Proceedings of Interspeech 2009, Brighton, England*. 20, 70

Rumelhart, D. and McClelland, J. (1987). Learning the past tenses of English verbs: Implicit rules or parallel distributed processing. *Mechanisms of language acquisition*, pages 195–248. 40, 41

Saffran, J. R., Newport, E. L., and Aslin, R. N. (1996). Word segmentation: The role of ditributional cues. *Journal of Memory and Language*, **35**, 606–621. DOI: 10.1006/jmla.1996.0032 49

Sagae, K., Davis, E., Lavie, A., MacWhinney, B., and Wintner, S. (2010). Morphosyntactic annotation of CHILDES transcripts. *Journal of Child Language*, **37**(03), 705–729. DOI: 10.1017/S0305000909990407 20

Sakas, W. and Fodor, J. (2001). The structural triggers learner. *Language acquisition and learnability*, pages 172–233. DOI: 10.1017/CBO9780511554360.006 47

Saxton, M. (2000). Negative evidence and negative feedback: Immediate effects on the grammaticality of child speech. *First Language*, **20**(60), 221. DOI: 10.1177/014272370002006001 45

Schachter, F. F. (1979). *Everyday mother talk to toddlers: Early intervention*. Academic Press. 26, 27

Schafer, G. and Mareschal, D. (2001). Modeling infant speech sound discrimination using simple associative networks. *Infancy*, **2**(1), 7–28. DOI: 10.1207/S15327078IN0201_2 28

Schone, P. and Jurafsky, D. (2001). Knowledge-free induction of inflectional morphologies. In *Second meeting of the North American Chapter of the Association for Computational Linguistics on Language Technologies*, pages 1–9. Association for Computational Linguistics. DOI: 10.3115/1073336.1073360 40

Schütze, H. (1993). Part-of-speech induction from scratch. In *Proceedings of the 31st annual meeting on Association for Computational Linguistics*, pages 251–258. Association for Computational Linguistics Morristown, NJ, USA. DOI: 10.3115/981574.981608 43

Seidenberg, M. and MacDonald, M. (1999). A probabilistic constraints approach to language acquisition and processing. *Cognitive Science*, **23**(4), 569–588. DOI: 10.1207/s15516709cog2304_8 69

Shayan, S. and Gershkoff-Stowe, L. (2007). How do children learn Agent and Patient roles? In *Poster presentation at SRCD Biennial Meeting Boston, Massachusetts, USA*. 62

Shi, R., Werker, J., and Morgan, J. (1999). Newborn infants' sensitivity to perceptual cues to lexical and grammatical words. *Cognition*, **72**(2), 11–21. DOI: 10.1016/S0010-0277(99)00047-5 42

Siskind, J. M. (1996). A computational study of cross-situational techniques for learning word-to-meaning mappings. *Cognition*, **61**, 39–91. DOI: 10.1016/S0010-0277(96)00728-7 29, 31, 33, 34

Slobin, D. I. (1973). Cognitive prerequisites for the development of grammar. In D. I. Slobin and C. A. Ferguson, editors, *Studies of child language development*, pages 175–208. Holt, Rinehart and Winston, New York. 1

Smith, L. B. (2000). Learning how to learn words: An associative crane. In R. M. Golinkoff and K. Hirsh-Pasek, editors, *Becoming a word learner: A debate on lexical acquisition*, pages 51–80. Oxford University Press. 27

Smith, L. B. and Yu, C. (2007). Infants rapidly learn words from noisy data via cross-situational statistics. In *Proceedings of the 29th Annual Conference of the Cognitive Science Society*. 27

Smith, L. B., Jones, S. S., Landau, B., Gershkoff-Stowe, L., and Samuelson, L. (2002). Object name learning provides on-the-job training for attention. *Psychological Science*, **13**(1), 13–19. DOI: 10.1111/1467-9280.00403 26

Solan, Z., Horn, D., Ruppin, F., and Edelman, S. (2004). Unsupervised context sensitive language acquisition from a large corpus. In L. Saul, editor, *Advances in Neural Information Processing*, volume 16. Cambridge, MA, MIT Press. 51

Solan, Z., Horn, D., Ruppin, E., and Edelman, S. (2005). Unsupervised learning of natural languages. *Proceedings of the National Academy of Sciences*, **102**(33), 11629–11634. DOI: 10.1073/pnas.0409746102 36

Sperber, D. (1994). The modularity of thought and the epidemiology of representations. *Mapping the mind: Domain specificity in cognition and culture*, pages 39–67. DOI: 10.1017/CBO9780511752902.003 2

Stager, C. L. and Werker, J. F. (1997). Infants listen for more phonetic detail in speech perception than in word learning tasks. *Nature*, **388**, 381–382. DOI: 10.1038/41102 26

Stolcke, A. and Omohundro, S. M. (1994). Inducing probabilistic grammars by Bayesian model merging. In *Proceedings of the Second International Colloquium on Grammatical Inference and Applications*, pages 106–118, London, UK. Springer-Verlag. 51

Stroppa, N. and Yvon, F. (2005). An analogical learner for morphological analysis. In *Proceedings of the 9th Conference on Computational Natural Language Learning*, pages 120–127. DOI: 10.3115/1706543.1706565 40

Swier, R. and Stevenson, S. (2004). Unsupervised semantic role labelling. In *Proceedings of the 2004 Conference on Empirical Methods in Natural Language Processing, Barcelona, Spain*, pages 95–102. 63

Taatgen, N. and Anderson, J. (2002). Why do children learn to say 'broke'? A model of learning the past tense without feedback. *Cognition*, **86**(2), 123–155. DOI: 10.1016/S0010-0277(02)00176-2 41

Tanenhaus, M., Spivey-Knowlton, M., Eberhard, K., and Sedivy, J. (1995). Integration of visual and linguistic information in spoken language comprehension. *Science*, **268**(5217), 1632. DOI: 10.1126/science.7777863 2, 23

Tenenbaum, J., Griffiths, T., and Kemp, C. (2006). Theory-based Bayesian models of inductive learning and reasoning. *Trends in Cognitive Sciences*, **10**(7), 309–318. DOI: 10.1016/j.tics.2006.05.009 19

Thompson, S. and Newport, E. (2007). Statistical learning of syntax: The role of transitional probability. *Language Learning and Development*, **3**(1), 1–42. DOI: 10.1207/s15473341lld0301_1 49

Tomasello, M. (2000). Do young children have adult syntactic competence? *Cognition*, **74**, 209–253. DOI: 10.1016/S0010-0277(99)00069-4 2, 4, 48, 62

Tomasello, M. (2003). *Constructing a language: A usage-based theory of language acquisition*. Harvard University Press. 2, 18, 48

Tomasello, M., Akhtar, N., Dodson, K., and Rekau, L. (1997). Differential productivity in young children's use of nouns and verbs. *Journal of Child Language*, **24**(02), 373–387. DOI: 10.1017/S0305000997003085 41

Toutanova, K. and Cherry, C. (2009). A global model for joint lemmatization and part-of-speech prediction. In *Proceedings of the 47th annual meeting of the Association for Computational Linguistics*, pages 486–494. Association for Computational Linguistics. DOI: 10.3115/1687878.1687947 40

Trueswell, J. C., Tanenhaus, M. K., and Garnsey, S. M. (1994). Semantic influences on parsing: Use of thematic role information in syntactic ambiguity resolution. *Journal of Memory and Language*, **33**(3), 285–318. DOI: 10.1006/jmla.1994.1014 62

Valiant, L. (1984). A theory of the learnable. *Communications of the ACM*, **27**(11), 1134–1142. DOI: 10.1145/1968.1972 46

van Zaanen, M. (2000). ABL: Alignment-based learning. In *Proceedings of the 18th conference on Computational Linguistics*, pages 961–967, Morristown, NJ, USA. Association for Computational Linguistics. 51

VanValin, R. D. and LaPolla, R. J. (1997). *Syntax: Structure, meaning and function*. Cambridge: Cambridge University Press. 62

Wacholder, N. (1995). *Syntactic Learning from Positive Evidence: An HPSG Model*. Ph.D. thesis, Ph. D. dissertation, City University of New York. 47

Werker, J., Fennell, C., Corcoran, K., and Stager, C. (2002). Infants' ability to learn phonetically similar words: Effects of age and vocabulary size. *Infancy*, **3**(1), 1–30. DOI: 10.1207/15250000252828226 26

Wicentowski, R. and Yarowsky, D. (2003). *Modeling and learning multilingual inflectional morphology in a minimally supervised framework*. Ph.D. thesis, The Johns Hopkins University. 40

Woodward, A. M., Markman, E. M., and Fitzsimmons, C. M. (1994). Rapid word learning in 13- and 18-month-olds. *Developmental Psychology*, **30**(4), 553–566. DOI: 10.1037/0012-1649.30.4.553 26

Xu, F. and Tenenbaum, J. B. (2007). Word learning as Bayesian inference. *Psychological Review*, **114**(2), 245–272. DOI: 10.1037/0033-295X.114.2.245 34

Yang, C. (2002). *Knowledge and learning in natural language*. Oxford University Press, USA. 47, 48

Yu, C. (2005). The emergence of links between lexical acquisition and object categorization: A computational study. *Connection Science*, **17**(3–4), 381–397. DOI: 10.1080/09540090500281554 29, 36, 37

Yu, C. (2006). Learning syntax–semantics mappings to bootstrap word learning. In *Proceedings of the 28th Annual Conference of the Cognitive Science Society*. 36

Yu, C. and Ballard, D. (2007). A unified model of early word learning: Integrating statistical and social cues. *Neurocomputing*, **70**(13-15), 2149–2165. DOI: 10.1016/j.neucom.2006.01.034 20, 37

Yu, C. and Smith, L. (2006). Statistical cross-situational learning to build word-to-world mappings. In *Proceedings of the 28th annual meeting of the cognitive science society*. Citeseer. 21